Sheffield and Peak District Walks

30 Favourite Walks

(Volume 1)

By
Stephen Murfitt

This book is dedicated to:

My lovely wife Andrea who I first met whilst on a Group walk and who has encouraged and supported me with my Group walking endeavours ever since. When I was first thinking of putting this book together and wasn't sure if I could write a book, she couldn't have been more encouraging and has been ever ready with advice throughout the many hours spent writing, choosing photos, and drawing maps. Thanks for everything sweetie!

Steve Murfitt

Copyright. © Stephen Murfitt 2021

All Rights Reserved. No part of this publication may be reproduced, stored, duplicated, or transmitted in any form or by any means – electronic, photocopy or otherwise without written permission by the publisher or author. Recording of this publication is strictly prohibited.

Printed by Mensa Printers Ltd, 323 Abbeydale Rd, Sheffield S7 1FS

Published by Independent Publishing Network

ISBN: 9781800494213

Front Cover Photograph: Rivelin Valley

Back Cover Photograph: Mayfield Valley

Maps & Photographs: Stephen Murfitt

Maps are provided only as a guide and are not necessarily to scale.

Disclaimer: The information in this book is given in good faith and is believed to be correct at the time of publication. No responsibility is accepted either by the author or the printer for errors or admissions, or for any loss or injury howsoever caused. Only you can judge your own fitness, competence and experience when undertaking any of the walks.

Sheffield and Peak District Walking Group have created and provided the routes and information for all the walks.

Thanks to Caroline Haynes for all her advice and help with the putting together of this book, and to Darren Haynes for his help also.

Thanks also to Nick and Su Gardner, and Nicky and Chris Rollings, for encouraging me to start the Sheffield and Peak District Group, and for being willing members of the author's 'recce posse', happily helping him to get lost on many an occasion!

Feedback on this book would be welcome. Please email Stephen Murfitt at sheffieldandpeakdistrictwalks@gmail.com

Foreword

For a good number of years, I have been involved in group walking. First of all by being a group member, and then for the last 14 years by arranging and leading walks for a number of local groups on a regular basis. Over time, using the walks that I have put together, I have managed to build up a large collection of walks which I have led for these groups, some of them in Sheffield and South Yorkshire, but the majority in Derbyshire.

During 2020 and 2021 however my group walk leading has been very much stop/start due to the lockdowns introduced because of the pandemic. Also during this period, due to the advice to walk locally, the areas in which I have been permitted to lead walks has had to change. No longer allowed to take my Sheffield-based group into Derbyshire, by late Summer 2020 I realised that I did not have enough Sheffield walks to be able to offer 2 different walks a week in our city, so I now had to look for new walks within my tier area, which basically meant in Sheffield and Rotherham.

Living close to Hillsborough, I started looking at areas near where I live such as Bradfield, Grenoside and Worrall and was pleasantly surprised to find places to walk which I had overlooked in the past. Furthermore, after I had 'walked the walks' I found that they were just as interesting as the more popular places that I normally lead walks in, and before too long, after lots of midweek jaunts with my 'recce friends' very quickly I was able to add a lot more Sheffield routes to my collection.

Which brings me round to the reason that I decided to write this book. In January 2021, the latest lockdown found me at a bit of a loose end, and basically looking for some sort of project to do. So when a friend sent me a recipe book she had created I had a sudden light bulb moment! Why not put all my favourite walks into a book, and especially as I had lots of new Sheffield walks to go along with my Derbyshire ones, try and aim to have half from each area?

Deciding on a name for the book was easy. Our group is the Sheffield and Peak District Walking Group, so it was a no-brainer for the book to be called

Sheffield and Peak District Walks – 30 Favourite Walks. Added to this, when I researched online what other walking books were available, it further emphasised to me that that it would be good to have Sheffield in the title as I found that there were very few books available of walks in the Sheffield area. Now deciding which walks to include in this book was another matter. For instance I deliberated for a while as to whether a Wentworth walk ought to be included, as Wentworth's not in Sheffield. But the walk I've been doing there for donkey's years is an absolute cracker, so in it went! Anyway, Wentworth's only 2 miles from the Sheffield boundary so who cares! Some favourite places had to be left out though, such as the Porter Valley, Mayfield Valley, Back Tor and Birley Edge. Perhaps they might be included in a second volume if that should ever happen.

For the format of the book, I have tried to make it as simple as possible to use by providing a description of the walk at the start of each chapter, followed by a map and an idea of how difficult the walk might be. After that there's the starting point and the route details, followed by details of interesting places to look out for en route and my opinion of how suitable the walk might be for dog owners, before finishing off with details of where it's possible to obtain refreshments.

I hope you enjoy reading about my 30 favourite walks and try some of them out and enjoy them just as much as I do. And if you ever fancy trying one of our group walks, there is more information about the types of walks we do, when they normally take place and how to contact us further on in the book. Please also feel free to email to let me know what you think of the book, and if you do decide to join us on a group walk, you'll be made very welcome indeed. Hope to see you soon!

Steve

Contents

Page No.

Walk No 1: Froggatt Edge	9 miles	9
Walk No 2: Blue Loop	4 miles	14
Walk No 3: Higgar Tor	4.5 miles	19
Walk No 4: Wentworth	7 miles	24
Walk No 5: Hope Valley	9 miles	29
Walk No 6: Greno Woods	4 miles	34
Walk No 7: Langsett	7 miles	38
Walk No 8: Millhouses	4.5 miles	42
Walk No 9: Loxley Valley	7.5 miles	46
Walk No 10: Padley Gorge	4 miles	51
Walk No 11: Lodge Moor	5 miles	55
Walk No 12: Norfolk Heritage	4.5 miles	60
Walk No 13: Stanage and Moscar	8.25 miles	65
Walk No 14: Hathersage Booths	4.5 miles	69
Walk No 15: Redmires	4 miles	74
Walk No 16: Worrall	7.5 miles	78
Walk No 17: Shatton Moor	7 miles	83
Walk No 18: Burbage Moor	4.5 miles	87
Walk No 19: Our Cow Molly	8 miles	92
Walk No 20 Blacka Moor	4 miles	97
Walk No 21: Eyam	8 miles	101
Walk No 22: Oaking Clough	5.25 miles	106
Walk No 23: Lost Villages	7.5 miles	110
Walk No 24: Rivelin Valley	4.5 miles	114
Walk No 25: Strines	7 miles	118
Walk No 26: Brookfield Manor	4.5 miles	123
Walk No 27: Chatsworth	7.5 – 8 miles	128
Walk No 28: Wyming Brook	4 miles	133
Walk No 29: Win Hill	7 miles	137
Walk No 30: Bradfield	4.75 miles	142

Map Legend

– – – –>	Walk route
△	Place of interest
■	Starting point
▭▬▭▬▭	Railway line
☐	Other building
⬬	Reservoir, dam or lake
✻	Viewpoint
▬▬▬▬	River
────	Other path
🌲	Woodland
▨	Grassed area

Walk No 1: Froggatt Edge & The River Derwent

9 miles/5 hours

Introduction

This walk combines two very different Peak District landscapes in the most dramatic of ways. Starting high up in the Dark Peak, the walk leads on to the first of three gritstone edges, Froggatt Edge, to be quickly followed by Curbar Edge and Baslow Edge before the route goes swiftly downhill to the River Derwent and into the White Peak. Before this though enjoy the superb views from the top of the edges of the lovely villages down below, and at the end of this moorland promenade the magnificent splendour of the Chatsworth estate in the distance. Before the descent though it's worth taking a look at the strange Eagle Stone rock formation, and learn the history of the Wellington's Monument, also high up on the gritstone edge. Then after a walk through the lovely village of Baslow it's riverside paths alongside the River Derwent as the river meanders its way through Calver Mill and the picturesque village of Froggatt on its way to Grindleford. At this point the river is left behind to tackle a steep(ish) hill climb through Haywood to return to the start.

Eagle Stone with Highland cattle and their young

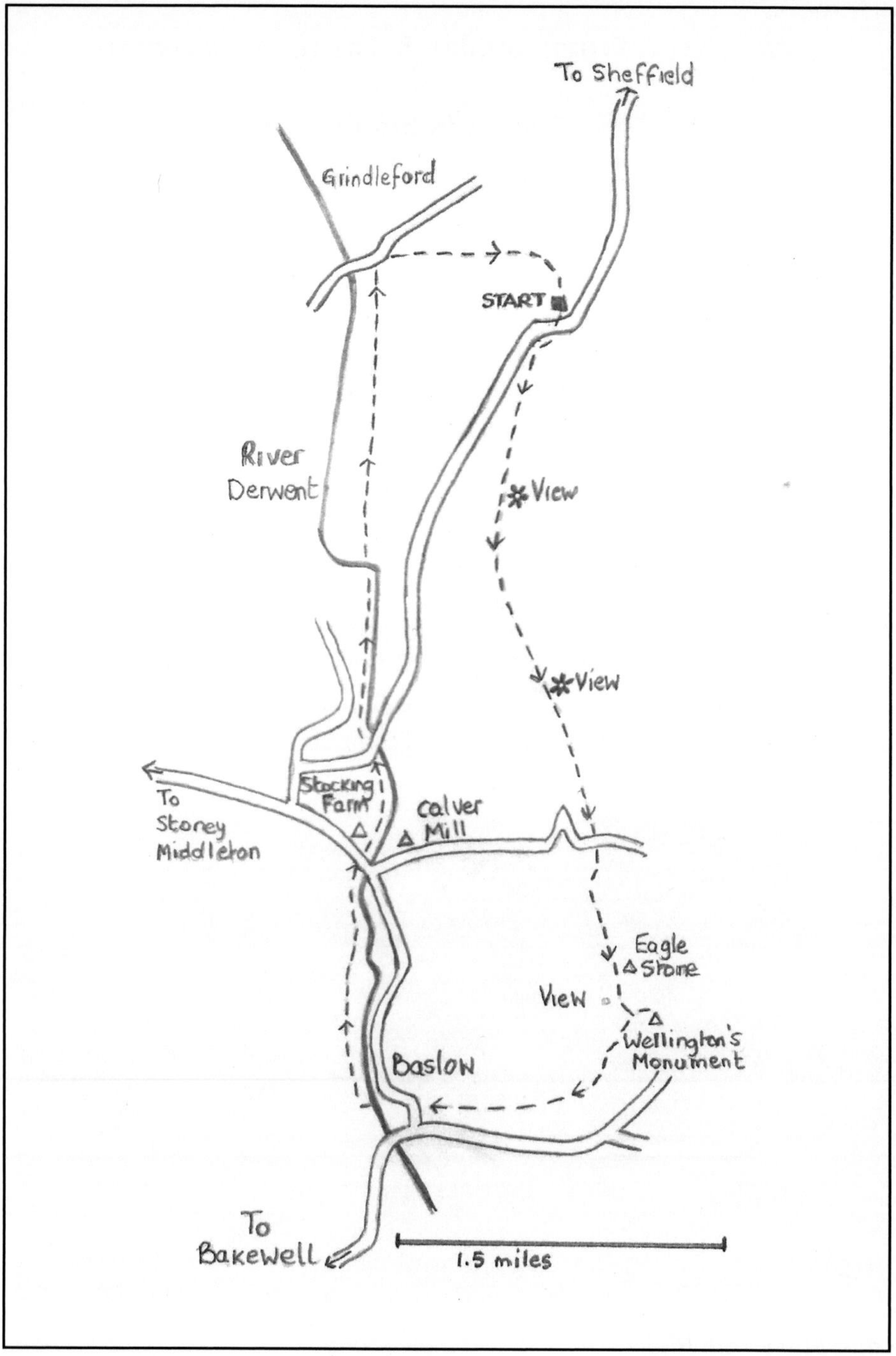
To Sheffield
Grindleford
START
River
Derwent
View
View
Stocking
Farm
To
Stoney
Middleton
Calver
Mill
Eagle
Stone
View
Wellington's
Monument
Baslow
To
Bakewell
1.5 miles

Walk Difficulty

At just over 9 miles in length and with quite a steep climb this walk is really only suitable for experienced walkers, although due to the lack of stiles, and the paths being fairly good throughout, it is a walk that shouldn't give regular walkers too much trouble. Watch out for cattle on top of the edges as there have been recent incidents with dog-owning walkers where the cattle have had calves, and obviously great care must be taken when walking next to the edges and alongside the river. There will also be a good deal of mud throughout the walk both in winter and after heavy rain.

Starting Point

The walk starts in the National Trust Pay-and-Display car park at Haywood just off the A625 between Wooden Pole junction and Froggatt village. The car park is situated just below the Grouse Inn on the same side of the road, and the postcode is S32 3ZJ. The walk could also be started from a free car parking area next to the Grouse Inn if there are parking spaces.

The Route

Leave the car park through a path at the bottom to head towards the road via a dip and a stream. At the road go right for 30 yards, then take the path on the left to walk along Froggatt Edge. The path stays close to the edge for 2.25 miles as Froggatt Edge becomes Curbar Edge, and the path reaches Clodhall Lane. Cross the lane and go through a gate on to a wide track. To enjoy the views from Baslow Edge bear right on to a rocky path which goes along the edge. This path re-joins the main path further on. After passing the Eagle Stone at 0.75 miles, bear left to visit Wellington's Monument.

Return to the path, and then turn right to take a track downhill towards the village of Baslow. The path bends a few times before after 0.75 miles it becomes a road. Further down at a grass triangle go straight ahead on to School Road to reach the main road at the bottom. Turn right, then cross the road to take a road on the left over a bridge. At the other side of the bridge turn right along Bubnell Lane for just over half a mile. As the road bends left, take a path on the right to cross a field, and then in a second field the path keeps to the right edge before it reaches the River Derwent.

Stay on this path alongside the river until it reaches Calver Bridge at the side of some houses. Cross the road, and the grass opposite to turn left along a service road for a few yards before turning right along the lane just after Calver Mill Gallery. At Stocking Farm bear right on to a path which crosses a field to reach the river. Stay on this path next to the river until after half a mile it emerges on to the A625.

Cross the road to take a path opposite which soon crosses a small bridge and stays to the left of the river to reach Froggatt Bridge after ½ mile. Go over the bridge then turn left to walk through Froggatt village along Hollowgate, which further on becomes Spooner Lane, which itself soon becomes a track. The track turns into a path further on but is still known as Spooner Lane.

After going through a squeeze stile, at a waymark bear half right to a wall gap, then go half left along a wall to cross a field to enter Horse Hay Wood. Leaving the wood, the path follows a wall to cross a stream and then heads through a field towards a road with Grindleford on the left. Turn right along the road, then after a few yards take a track on the right just before the church. After the track bends right, follow the sign for Froggatt Edge on to a path which initially climbs beside a wall. As the path goes through woodland cross another path, and then higher up, bear right to join a wide path that climbs gradually across the hillside. This path leads to the car park.

Look out for…..

Outstanding Views all the way along all three edges. The villages of Eyam, Stoney Middleton and Calver can be seen early in the walk, and then at Baslow Edge, Chatsworth House and grounds including the fountains can be seen by looking over to the left.

Eagle Stone on Baslow Edge. The Eagle Stone is said to have come from the Norse god Aigle, who had a reputation for throwing large rocks around, and it is said to turn or move on certain days of the year. It is also the site of where, in times past, the young men of Baslow would prove their worth to the women of the village, by climbing the stone (there is a fairly easy way up!).

Wellington's Monument also on Baslow Edge. The monument is dedicated to the Duke of Wellington and a celebration of his victory at the battle of Waterloo in 1815. It was erected by a local. called Dr Wrench, who as an army man felt the need to counterbalance the memorial dedicated to Admiral Nelson on nearby Birchen Edge.

Calver Mill was built in 1778 by John Gardom of Bakewell and John Pares of Leicester. In 1799 the River Derwent washed away Calver Bridge and took part of the mill with it. Shortly after this event, the mill was burned to the ground. A new mill was subsequently built and began production in 1804 and by 1830 it employed 200 workers. Spinning finished in 1923, but during World War 2 the mill was used as a storage depot and as a plant for crushing and washing fluorspar used in steelmaking.

Stocking Farm School at Calver Bridge. The Factory Act of 1833 required that schools be provided for children working in the mills, and every child between 9 and 13 years was given a certificate each week to say that they had "been schooled" for two hours each day. Calver Cotton Mill was no exception, and they provided a schoolroom for their child workers in an upper room of a barn belonging to the Stocking Farm, which they also owned. The mill owner also summoned a doctor on a monthly basis to call to check the children's health with regard to "cotton fibres in the lungs".

Dog Suitability

A 9 mile walk with hardly any stiles is always a good thing for dog owners, and there are quite long stretches where dogs can be off lead. An eye must be kept open though for the above-mentioned cattle and also sheep, particularly on Baslow Edge where the cattle seem to congregate. In the fields alongside the River Derwent there could be sheep as well.

Refreshments

In Baslow there are pubs and shops for food and drink, and the church café at Grindleford may also be open, depending what time of day it is. There is also the Grouse Inn at the start/end of the walk.

Walk No 2: Blue Loop (Five Weirs and Canal)
4 miles/2 hours

Introduction

Sheffield City Centre is full of surprises, and there are quite a few of them on this interesting walk, which is close to the city centre, yet well off the beaten track. Combining parts of the Blue Loop Five Weirs/canal walk with the Upper Don Trail, the route offers a good look at a number of iconic places which many people will probably heard of but never seen! These include Salmon Pastures at Attercliffe, the spot on the canal where a scene from the Full Monty was filmed, colourful barges in the canal basin, the Dorothy Pax, Sheffield Castle, Sheffield's Nicaraguan Esteli Parade, Kelham Island, the grade II listed Royal Exchange flats on the Wicker, Lady's Bridge, Cobweb Bridge, and a Normandy Landings Bailey Bridge.

1858 Bessemer Converter outside Kelham Island museum

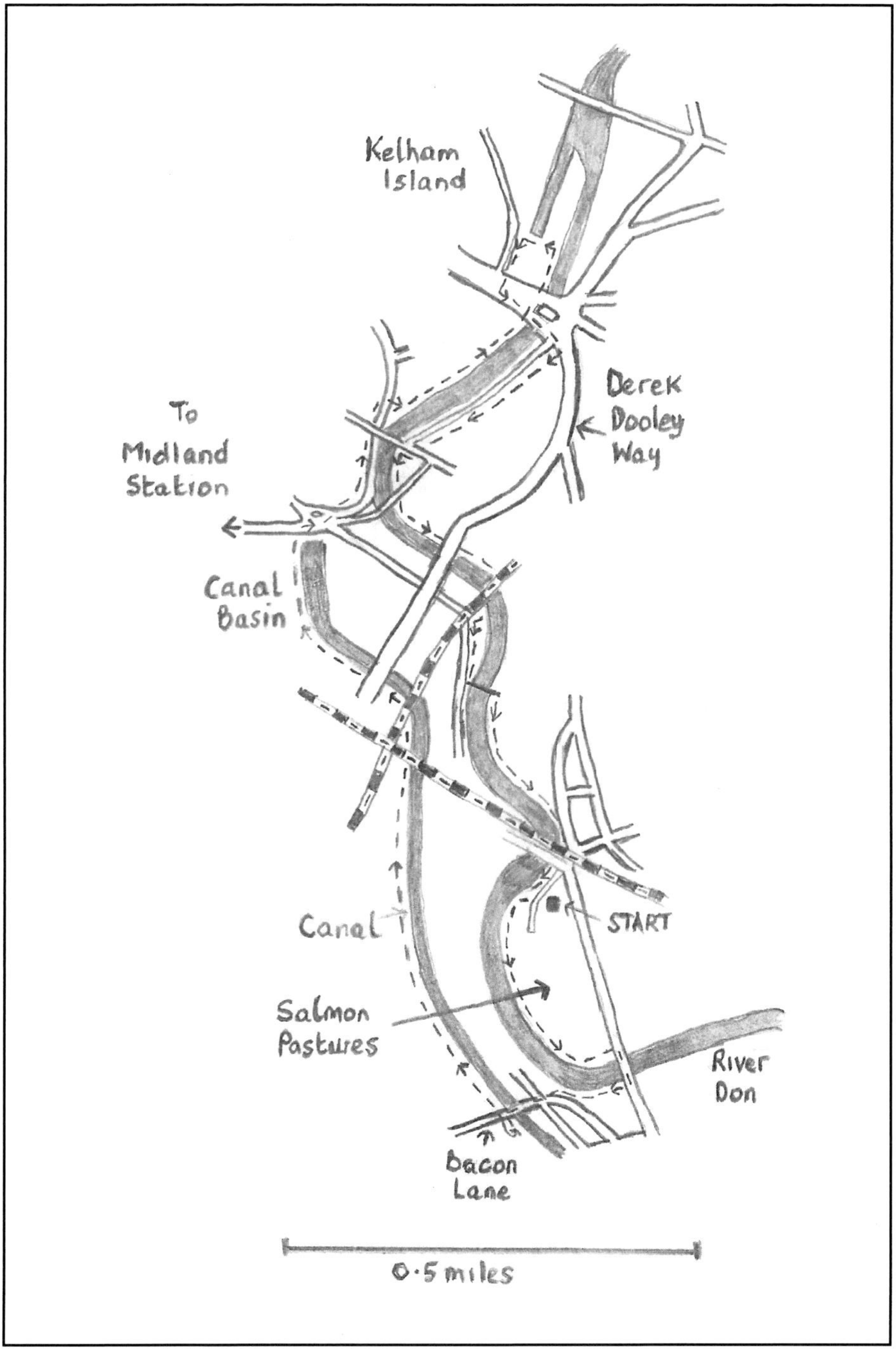
Kelham Island
Derek Dooley Way
To Midland Station
Canal Basin
START
Canal
Salmon Pastures
River Don
Bacon Lane
0·5 miles

Walk Difficulty

This is an easy walk and suitable for all abilities as it takes place on mainly good, flat paths and has very few hazards along the way. There are two short stretches where the paths could be muddy in winter and after rain, and there are some busy roads to cross, but that's it!

Starting Point

The walk can be started anywhere on the route however because there is ample free parking, I have started the route details from Warren St, S4 7WT where there is access straight on to the Five Weirs path.

The Route

Take the signed path on Warren Street which leads to the river, and then heads away from the city centre. After ½ a mile leave the river to go up to Washford Bridge. Cross the bridge, then take a path immediately to the right which cuts through to Stoke Street. Keep right, then cross on to Bacon Lane opposite. Where the bridge crosses the canal, take the towpath on the left down to the canal then double back under the bridge towards the city centre. Keep on the towpath to Canal Basin.

Stay on the left side of the basin and leave it on to Exchange Street. Cross the road, turn right and then bear left on to Castlegate to cross over on to Bridge Street at the end. After 50 yards, take the path right through buildings to the river. Turn left and go as far as the ring road, where the path ends.

To have a look at Kelham Island, cross the two roads opposite and take a path to the right of Tesco. This emerges into Kelham Island near the museum. After a look at the museum and the general area turn left along Alma Road to return to the ring road, then cross back over to reach the road bridge.

For the shorter route, go right over the bridge (as will anybody returning from Kelham Island) then immediate right on to Nursery Street. At the footbridge take the ramp up to the bridge but do not cross over it, go straight ahead into a small park. Exit the park on to Nursery Street, then at the end cross the road to take a path at the end of the buildings. This is the start of the Five Weirs Walk.

At the end of the path cross Blonk Street to stay on the Five Weirs path which further on carries on over the Spider Bridge and on to a side road which leads to Furnival Road. Go left to walk along the road, then after about 400 yards cross the Bailey Bridge and stay on this path to Attercliffe Road. Turn right and then Warren Street is across the road at the first junction.

Look out for…..

Two of the Five Weirs. Burton Weir at the start of the walk and Walk Mill Weir just after passing over the Spider Bridge. Sanderson's Weir, Brightside Weir, Hadfields Weir are the other three weirs.

Salmon Pastures was so called because of the abundance of salmon in the early 1800's. The growth of industry in the area soon got rid of the fish although there are current plans for them to return. A school was built in 1908 on the site and was demolished in 1998. Latterly the school was an annex of Shirecliffe College. The Grey Horse pub was also on the site as was a chippie.

The Full Monty was filmed in lots of locations all over Sheffield, but one of the early scenes of the film was filmed on a section of the canal close to Bacon Lane.

Dorothy Pax was the name of the last working barge to be used at Victoria Quays. Built in 1913 the barge was used to bring coke into the city, and to take iron back out. By the 1970's the barge was no longer used to transport goods, and after a short life as a houseboat it was scrapped in the 2000's. In 2017 a new bar called Dorothy Pax was opened in the Canal Basin and named in honour of the barge.

Canal Basin or Victoria Quays as it's better-known dates from 1814, when the canal was built to connect with the River Don at Tinsley, allowing canal boats to reach the heart of Sheffield for the first time. When it opened on 22 February 1819 a general holiday was called and a crowd of 60,000 gathered to watch the first boats, a flotilla of 10 which arrived from Tinsley. Within the flotilla was one barge of coal brought from Handsworth Colliery – the first cargo to travel the canal.

Esteli Parade was opened in 2018 as a new cycle route and riverside path to celebrate 30 years of friendship with Sheffield's twin town in Nicaragua.

The Upper Don Trail will eventually link Sheffield city centre to the Peak District. Starting from the site of Sheffield's historic castle, it threads its way through Kelham Island, Parkwood Springs Country Park and Wardsend Cemetery to cross Penistone Road at Wadsley Bridge. Then it's on to Claywheels Lane before entering Beeley Wood on its way to Oughtibridge. Further along, after passing Wharncliffe Crags at Wharncliffe Side the trail will follow the Little Don at Deepcar to carry on through Fox Valley to Stocksbridge, Langsett and the famous Cut Gate trail into the Peak District.

Cobweb Bridge or Spider Bridge is 100 metres long and was built in 2002. It was designed by Sheffield City Council's Structures Section and it solved the problem of continuing the Five Weir Walk under the Wicker Arches viaduct.

Dog Suitability

There are two sections where dogs can be off lead but for the most part they will have to be led.

Refreshments

At the Canal Basin there is the Victoria Basin café and the Dorothy Pax bar. There are also numerous interesting café's, bars and pubs at Kelham Island and various eating and drinking places in The Wicker area.

Bacon Lane bridge on the canal in winter

Walk No 3: Higgar Tor

4.5 miles/2.5 hours

Introduction

Higgar Tor is a dominant landmark in the Dark Peak, and lies within the Sheffield border. It is an extremely popular place for walking, due to it being easily accessible from several different directions, with the rewards for getting up there being great views in every direction. As well as the views, other features of this walk are a delightful section next to Burbage Brook, the Mother Cap rock formation, and Carl Wark another rock formation which has a 2500-year history, and the stunning Burbage Valley!

Walking Group with Carl Wark and Higgar Tor in the background

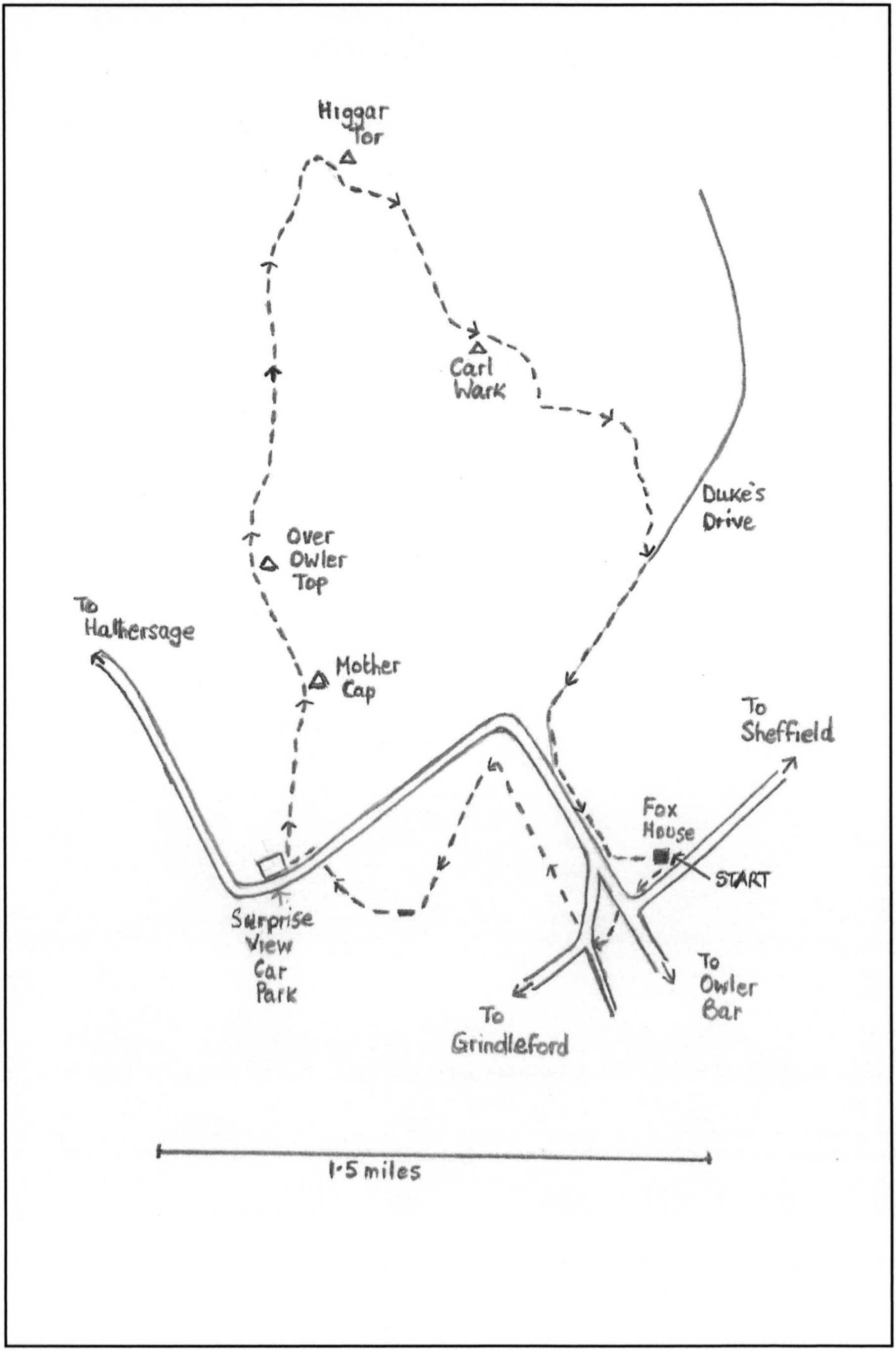
Higgar Tor
Carl Wark
Duke's Drive
Over Owler Top
To Hathersage
Mother Cap
To Sheffield
Fox House
START
Surprise View Car Park
To Owler Bar
To Grindleford
1·5 miles

Walk Difficulty

This is quite a hilly walk and includes a difficult section through rocks so it would be better suited to experienced walkers. After rain and in Winter, there is the usual mud and standing water, and there is a section just after passing Carl Wark which is always boggy, even in Summer.

Starting Point

The car park at the Fox House pub has been chosen for the start of this walk although it could also be started at Surprise View car park. The first car park at the Fox House is a public one, but the one behind it is for Fox House customers only. There is also parking alongside the A625. The pub address is The Fox House Hathersage Rd, Sheffield S11 7TY

The Route

Turn right to come out of the Fox House car park then as the road bends right cross over to go through a gate opposite which leads on to the Longshaw Estate. At the estate road turn right to the main road. Cross the road and go through a gate a few yards up the road which leads on to a path. Take this path and then fork left further on. After a couple of minutes after crossing a stream the path goes left downhill to cross a bridge over a river.

Over the bridge turn left to follow the river until just before another bridge there is a junction of paths. Take the first path to the right which leads through grass bankings to reach the A625 Hathersage Road. Cross the road and go through a gate to turn left towards the Surprise View car park. At the carpark go right through a gate just behind a Pay and Display machine.

The path goes half right up the hill towards trees and then once through the trees heads towards some large rocks and then up to the top of the hill to Mother Cap rock formation. Behind Mother Cap the path carries on in roughly the same direction towards and through more rocky outcrops to reach the highest point of this part of the walk, Over Owler Top. Pass slightly to the right of this rock formation and then after passing through a rocky section drop down on to a path which carries on through heather in the same direction towards Higgar Tor, which can be seen in the distance.

Eventually the path reaches a sheepfold which it goes to the left of, to carry on towards the left-hand side of Higgar Tor. As the path starts to climb there is a crossroad of paths where there are two options. The more strenuous option is to carry on upwards to climb through rocks to reach the top of Higgar Tor. The easier option is to turn right on to a narrow path which stays below Higgar Tor and which after 300 yards joins up with a wider path which leads right, towards Carl Wark. If taking the more difficult route, once at the top of Higgar Tor turn right and walk along the top, staying close to the edge to the far corner. There is a path there which leads down to the lower path. For a few minutes this will involve climbing through large boulders.

Once on the lower path turn left for a short while until the wider path is reached which heads towards Carl Wark. Just before the path climbs up to Carl Wark take a path left which leads downhill through a boggy area to a bridge over Burbage Brook. Over the bridge the path bends right to cross another bridge, and then leads to a footpath T junction. Turn right and stay on this path to reach the A625. Take a narrow path left which runs parallel to the road to start with, in the direction of the Fox House. After a while, the path leads away from the road to come out into the Fox House car park.

Look out for…..

Fox House was built in 1773 and is one of the highest pubs in Yorkshire at 1,132-foot above sea level. It was famous as a calling place for carrier carts and stagecoaches in the past, but equally so for illegally serving wagon drivers during "the small hours". Originally called "The Travellers Rest" it was later named after the Fox Family of Callow near Hathersage.

Higgar Tor is 200 metres inside the Sheffield border and at 1424 feet/434 metres above sea level is the highest point in the Peak District Eastern Moors. 200 metres inside the Sheffield border.

Carl Wark was thought to have been fortified in the Iron Age at the same time as Mam Tor. Later on in the Romano-British period at the start of the Dark Ages, massive fortifications were constructed and can still be seen at the western entrance.

The Burbage Valley can be seen throughout the second half of the walk and is part of the Longshaw Estate which since 1931 has been owned by the National Trust. Running through the middle of the valley is a wide path called Duke's Drive. The drive was so named after the Duke of Rutland when it was created for him to transport his guests to shoot grouse on the surrounding moors.

Dog Suitability

There is the possibility of sheep and cows throughout this walk, so the advice from the National Trust is to keep dogs on leads to protect the animals. This is especially so in the breeding season of 1st March to 31st July. The good news is that there are no stiles at all on this walk.

Refreshments

The Fox House is the only place to obtain refreshments on the route apart from ice cream vans often situated close to the Burbage Brook section and at Surprise View car park. The café at Longshaw Estate is only a 5-minute walk from the start/end of the walk.

Refreshment time at Surprise View

Walk No: 4 Wentworth Follies

7 miles/ 4 hours

Introduction

Not quite in Sheffield, but near enough to the city boundary to be included in this book, this walk is a must for all history lovers. Featuring two villages whose history is steeped in the 19c Industrial Revolution, the walk takes place almost entirely within the Fitwilliam Estate, with all its follies and of course Wentworth Woodhouse. Starting at the Elsecar Heritage Centre, which is worth an hour or two's visit on its own, the walk takes us past the Needle's Eye folly to the picturesque hamlet of Street. Two more follies then follow, the unusual three-sided Hoober Stand, and the Mausoleum on the way to Fitzwilliam's stately home, Wentworth Woodhouse. From there it's a nice wander through Wentworth village on the way back to the start.

Paradise Square, Wentworth

25

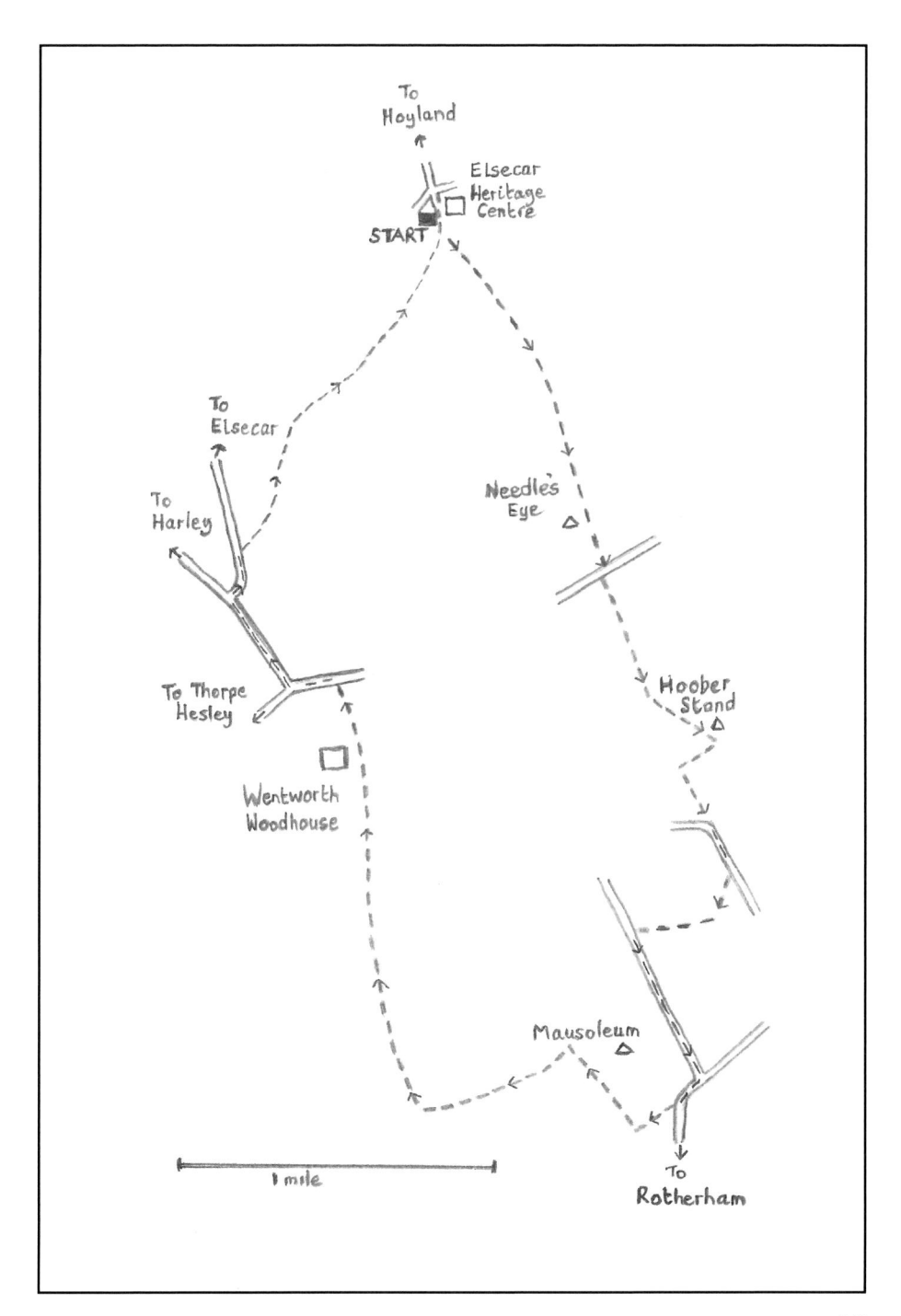

Walk Difficulty

This is a fairly easy walk really, however there are quite a few stiles to negotiate, and there are also one or sections where there could be a great deal of mud. Add to this a short sharp hill at the start, but apart from that it's quite a gentle stroll through this interesting part of Rotherham and Barnsley.

Starting Point

The starting point for the walk is the Elsecar Heritage Centre car park, Wentworth Road, Elsecar, S74 8EP. The walk could also be started in the centre of Wentworth although there is limited parking there.

The Route

From the entrance to the Heritage Centre go left along the lane, then entering the woods fork left on a path which leads to fields. Up a steep hill go through two fields to reach a path between fields at the top of the hill. After half a mile the path reaches a road just after passing the Needles Eye folly.

Cross the road, then take the road left, Street Lane. After passing the last house take a path left which cuts diagonally across a field towards a small wood. Go over a stile into the wood then take a path half left to head up to the Hoober Stand folly. With the entrance behind, take a path left for a few yards, and then go downhill on another path to the right. Reaching Street Lane again, turn left to walk on to Hoober Lane.

Go left on Hoober Lane for 100 yards to cross the road to go half left on a path through trees which leads to a field. At a hedge in the corner take a path right to keep the hedge on your left, then go through a gap in the hedge further down to keep in the same direction with the hedge now on the right. At Cortworth Lane turn left and walk on the other side of the road for half a mile, passing the entrance to the Mausoleum before reaching the main road.

Turn right and walk along Stubbin Road for 200 yards to take a path right between cottages. Turn right on to a path at the last house which leads on to the top of a field with woods on the right. Part way along this path there is a glimpse of the Mausoleum through the trees. At the end of the field the path heads downhill, and then cuts through a gap in the hedge on the right to go diagonally across a field. Here, the path carries on downhill with the hedge right, then at the bottom it crosses a stream to enter another field.

Head diagonally right across grass aiming for the far corner where the field ends at an estate road. Turn right to walk towards Wentworth Woodhouse, then with the house about 100 yards away take a path right which leads to another estate road. Stay on this road all the way to the top passing Wentworth Woodhouse, and the old stables on the left.

At the main road turn left to walk into Wentworth staying on the main road as it bends right to go through the village. Take time to look at the picturesque cottages in Paradise Square, and also both the new church and the ruins of the old church which are up a lane on the left. As the road bends left at the end of the village take a road right signposted to Elsecar. After a ¼ of a mile take a path right at Wentworth Sawmills. This track becomes a path and leads back to the start.

Look out for…..

Elsecar Heritage Centre is a living history centre. It covers the industrial history of the area, and includes a Newcomen Beam engine, the only such engine still in its original location in the country. It has its own goods station and steam engines and the centre also comprises shops, businesses, galleries, art and craft studios and an exhibition hall.

The Needles Eye is a 45ft high sandstone pyramid with an ornamental urn over a Gothic ogee arch. It was built in the mid-18th Century, allegedly to win a bet after the 1st Marquis claimed he could drive a coach and horses through the eye of a needle!

Hoober Stand is a 100ft tapering pyramid structure with a hexagonal lantern built by the 1st Marquis of Rockingham in 1747-8 to commemorate the defeat of the Jacobite rebellion.

The Mausoleum was built in 1783 by the 4th Earl Fitzwilliam in memory of his uncle Charles 2nd Marquis of Rockingham (whose body is actually in York Minster). It contains the busts of 8 great Whigs of the period, but no bodies!

Wentworth Woodhouse is Grade 1 listed and is owned by the Wentworth Woodhouse Preservation Trust. It has more than 300 rooms and has 250,000 square feet of floorspace. It covers an area of more than 2.5 acres. In 2016 the truest was awarded a Govt grant of £7.6m for restoration work.

Wentworth Village was recorded in the Domesday Book in 1066 and took its name from the Wentworth family who were local landowners. Through the middle ages the Woodhouse family, and then the Watson family had a great deal of influence in the area providing members of Parliament, and a Prime Minister. In the late 18c the Earl Fitzwilliams took over the estate and were responsible for much of the early industrial development in the area, establishing numerous mines and factories in the surrounding towns and villages. By the mid-nineteenth century they were reckoned to be the 6th wealthiest landowners in the country. They didn't lose touch with the village though and gave money to establish the Mechanics Institute and the girls school for the benefit of their tenants. They also built cottages for their workers in Wentworth and Elsecar, which still exist today.

Dog Suitability

Not the best of walks if you prefer your dog to be off-lead as there are three or four road sections, plus the estate road which is 'dogs-on-leads only'. The fields after leaving the Heritage Centre usually have horses in them too.

Refreshments

There are cafes at the Heritage Centre and a pub which doesn't seem to open much nor particularly cater for visitors needs, but if it's pubs with good food that you want then there are 2 to be recommended in Wentworth. There are also cafes and a takeaway shop in Wentworth.

The Needles Eye taken looking towards Wentworth Woodhouse. The author can just about be seen to the left of the folly!

Walk No: 5 Hope Valley

9 miles/4.5 hours

Introduction

Most walks in the Hope Valley include hills and ridges. This walk is different insomuch as it takes place at low-level along both sides of the valley from where there is the chance to appreciate the sheer beauty of the hills, whilst enjoying some of the lovely villages and hamlets that are away from the normal walk routes. Leaving from Bamford the walk passes through the villages of Shatton, Brough and Hope on the way to Castleton; then on the return leg its Hope again, followed by Aston and Thornhill. There is a mixture of farm tracks and field paths, as well as a bit of road walking and a lovely section alongside Peakshole Water.

The village of Hope with Lose Hill and Kinder Scout in the background

30

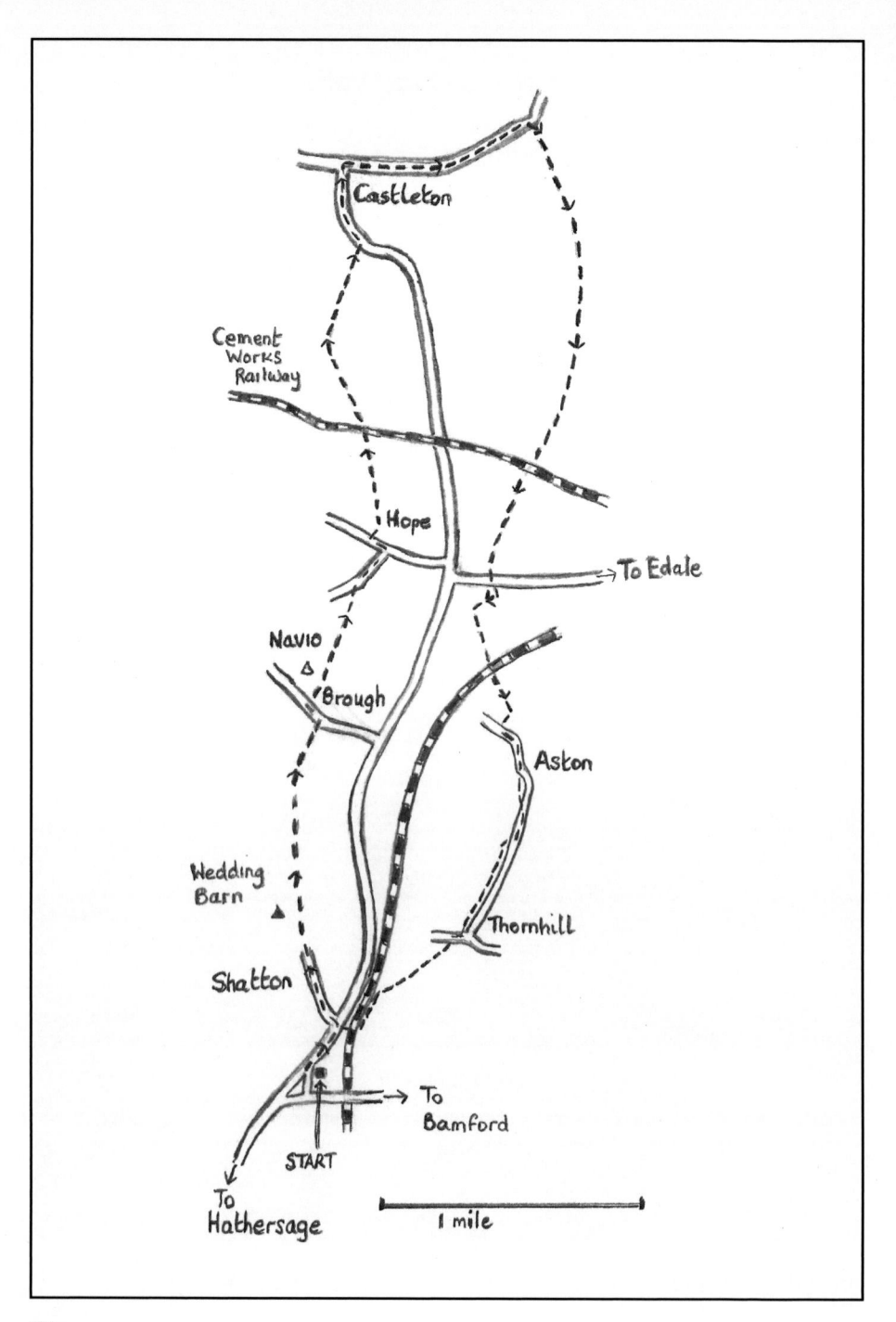

Walk Difficulty

With no hills and just a couple of short inclines this is a fairly easy 9 miler as far as Peak District walks go. There are quite a few stiles on the route though, and after rain the field paths can get muddy but apart from some road walking to be careful with, that's it!

Starting Point

The walk details start from the bottom of Mytham Bridge, which is a road, in Bamford. Postcode is S33 0EA. The walk could also be started in Hope or in Castleton. There is plenty of roadside parking at Mytham Bridge which makes it the perfect place to start the walk.

The Route

From Mytham Bridge turn right along the main road past the garden centre and cross the road to go over Shatton Bridge. Continue along Shatton Lane as it leaves the village, and after crossing a ford 100 yards further on go up steps on the left to take a path through a field which runs parallel to the lane. The path passes behind the wedding barn and returns to the lane further up. At Shatton Hall go right through a gate to carry on in the same direction on a path which enters woods before coming out on to Brough Lane.

Follow the lane down to the main road then turn left for a few yards to take a footpath opposite which leads into a field. Head diagonally right across the field to a ladder stile, then bear slightly left to walk along the top of the field alongside a fence. Further along, look for a path cutting across a banking to reach a grass track heading towards a road. At the road turn right to go down the road and keep going downhill to reach Pindale Road at the bottom.

Go left along the road and as it starts to climb uphill take a path on the right which skirts round a field, with trees and a drop down to the river on the right. Stay on this path close to the river for a while, but then after crossing a railway line it leaves the river to keep in the same direction, passing the Hope Valley Cement Works as it heads towards Castleton. Re-joining the river further on, the path carries on to eventually reach the main road.

Turn left and cross the road, staying on it until it bends left. At the bend, take the road on the right which passes between cottages on its way out of Castleton. After passing a cemetery on the right, fork right on to a lane which passes an Outward Bound Centre on the left, and a sports field on the right. Where the lane bends sharp left, go straight across on a path towards a wooded area. Through the woods keep in the same direction to reach a lane. Go on to the lane keeping in the same direction to pass the back of Losehill Hall on the right.

Further on, as the lane bends left towards a farm go straight on to reach houses and a farm lane. Turn left, then after a few yards take a path right in front of stables. Stay on this path in the same direction through gates and over stiles in fields as a path joins it from the left after which the path curls right to go through buildings, and then over a rail crossing.

After going through more fields go left at cross paths to reach Edale Road. Cross the road and turn left to take a fork right after a few yards. Cross the river then take a track right which stays close to the river then leads to buildings. Past the first house on the left take steps up to a field, then turn sharp right to bend right through two fields to a kissing gate.

Left here leads towards a railway bridge, which after passing under, the path leads right, and enters a field. Go half right across the field to reach a farm drive. Right here leads to Aston Lane. Turn left to go uphill and stay on the road as it bends right to go into Aston. As the road bends left go straight across on to a track which becomes a path as it goes past houses.

Keep straight forward until the path leads back to the road. Stay on the road until a path is reached on the right just after Highfield Head Farm. Take this path, then fairly quickly take another path left which runs parallel to the road staying on it until it re-joins the road, almost in Thornhill.

At Thornhill, at a 'T' junction go right, then immediately take a path left through trees. At the end of this path turn right to reach a lane at the bottom. Turn left along the lane, then after 50 yards take a path right to cross a field diagonally. Where the field ends, turn right to go under a railway bridge, then at the road turn left to return to the start.

Look out for…..

Mytham Bridge was the site of important toll gates built in 1758 to take payment from people using the main road from Sheffield to Sparrowpit.

Shatton means 'farmstead in the nook of land between streams', which describes this little settlement perfectly as it sits beside the confluence of the Derwent and Noe. Townfield Lane which leads away from Shatton is an ancient route which was part of a salters lane which ran from Sheffield to Cheshire.

Wedding Barn on Townfield Lane at Shatton. Great place for a wedding reception!

Navio Roman Fort was built in AD 73, 30 years after the Roman invasion. It was abandoned in AD 128 when all available troops were sent further north. A new fort was then built in AD 158. Situated in a flat, green field above a sharp bend in the River Noe, in latin the name Navio means "on the river" and the likelihood is that it was put there to guard a crossing point over the river.

Hope Valley Cement Works Railway line carries almost 1.5 million tonnes of cement annually on the 1.5-mile line which runs from the centre of the works to the mainline near Hope station. The cement works have their own diesel hydraulic locomotive *Blue John*.

Thornhill Trail is a path which leads from near the High Peak Garden Centre up to the Ladybower Dam. It is 2 miles long and is a former narrow gauge railway track which was built between 1935 and 1943 to take raw materials to the upper Derwent Valley for the construction of the Ladybower Dam.

Dog Suitability

There are a few decent stretches where dogs can be off lead, but for a good half of the walk there is either fields with sheep or there is road walking. There are quite a lot of stiles to tackle as well.

Refreshments

There are lots of pubs cafes and shops in Castleton plus the garden centre at the start of the walk.

Walk No: 6 Greno Woods Nature Reserve

4 miles / 2 hours

Introduction

Greno Woods Nature Reserve is situated on the outskirts of the village of Grenoside in the North of Sheffield. At over 300 acres, and with paths all over the place the Reserve makes a great place to walk, and this particular walk takes place almost entirely on good woodland paths and tracks making it suitable for most people. The route starts with a circuit of Greno Woods to the right of Woodhead Road before crossing over the road to walk through Wheata Wood and Prior Royd Wood to return to the start. Greno Woods has existed since 1600AD and is a peaceful ancient woodland with lots of wildlife to look out for including brown hares, badgers, bats and the rare shining guest ant.

Autumn scene in Greno Woods

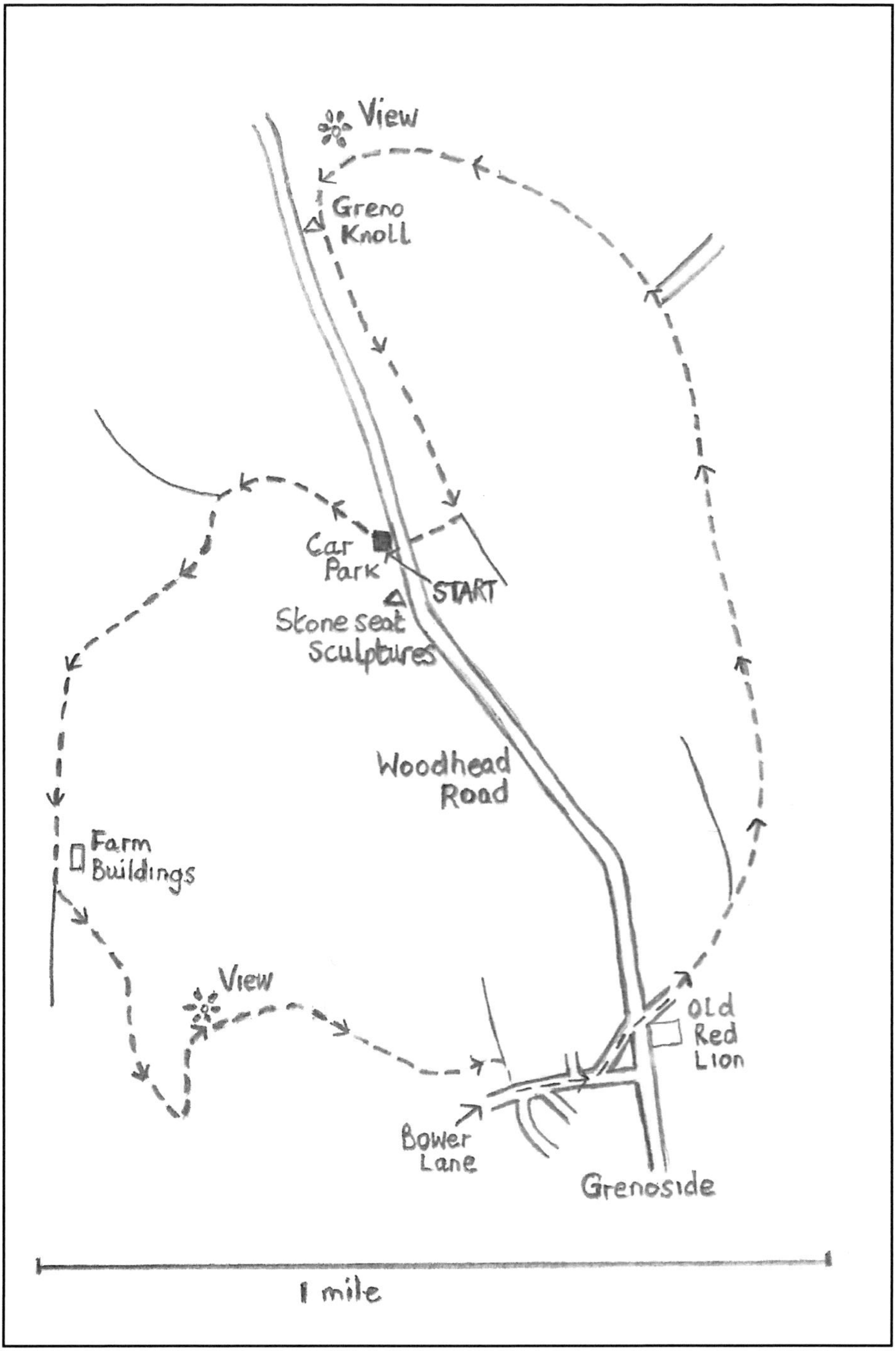
View
Greno Knoll
Car Park
START
Stone seat Sculptures
Woodhead Road
Farm Buildings
View
Old Red Lion
Bower Lane
Grenoside
1 mile

Walk Difficulty

There are a couple of short inclines as can be expected on most Sheffield walks, but very few other things to watch out for on this walk. Some mud can be expected after rain and there are always a few cyclists knocking about especially as part of the route is on a National Cycle Route there are no stiles at all which is always a bonus!

Starting Point

The starting point for the walk is Grenoside Wood car park, Woodhead Rd, Sheffield S35 8RS. The walk can also be started from the centre of Grenoside.

The Route

At the car park, take the track right to go downhill. After ½ mile go left at the fork, then after 0.4 miles take the second path left, just after farm buildings to cross a small stream. Ignore 2 paths left as the path starts to climb to reach cross paths. Turn left here to double back and stay on the path as it continues to climb, ignoring paths left and right. A junction of paths is reached at the top close to a wall with a field behind it on the right. Take the path right to stay close to the edge of the woods to start with, with the wall on the right, before the path joins a main path coming from the left before bending right to come out on to Bower Lane.

Turn left to walk down the road then take the second road left, Cupola Lane. This leads to Main Street almost opposite The Old Red Lion pub (known as 'Top Red' locally. Turn left to walk along the road for about 50 yards then cross over to go right along a lane which is behind the pub. Where the houses end the lane becomes a path into Greno Woods. After 350 yards bear right at a fork and then stay on this wide path ignoring all paths left and right.

After half a mile the path passes the top of a track and soon after goes uphill whilst bending to the left. At the top of the hill, just before the road, take the path which goes sharp left, then after about ¼ mile take the path right. Cross the road to take a path opposite slightly to the right. The path heads left to return to the car park.

Look out for…..

Seat sculptures. There are 2 stone seat sculptures by the artist-craftsman Ian Boyle quite close to the car park in Wheata Wood.

Greno Knoll. This is the highpoint in the Grenoside area at 312 metres, 1024 feet above sea level and is marked by a trig point.

Bird life. In winter there are redwings, fieldfare, siskins, redpolls, bramblings and various types of tits. In summer, migrant warblers such as blackcaps, chiffchaffs, willow warblers can also be seen. Other rarely seen birds that can be spotted all year round include nuthatch, sparrowhawks and lesser-spotted woodpeckers, linnets and little owls.

Dog Suitability

A great walk for dog owners whose dogs can be off lead throughout all three woodland areas. No stiles on this one either.

Refreshments

In Grenoside village there are several pubs, and also a village shop.

Stone seat sculpture in Wheata Woods

Walk No: 7 Langsett

7 miles / 4 hours

Introduction

This walk is probably most suitable for experienced walkers due to the ruggedness of the paths. It includes many interesting features such as an almost full circuit of Langsett Dam, the hamlet of Upper Midhope, the village of Midhopestones and the ruins of the North America farmstead. The walk takes place mainly on farm tracks and permissive paths, and is entirely within South Yorkshire, with half of it being in Sheffield, and half in Barnsley. Interestingly half of the walk is in the Peak District, and half of it not! There are great views throughout the walk which includes a total ascent of 1000 feet, and has a couple of historical features, the ancient Langsett Barn and a disused railway line which was built for the construction of the dam.

Langsett Dam with Hartcliffe Hill in the background.

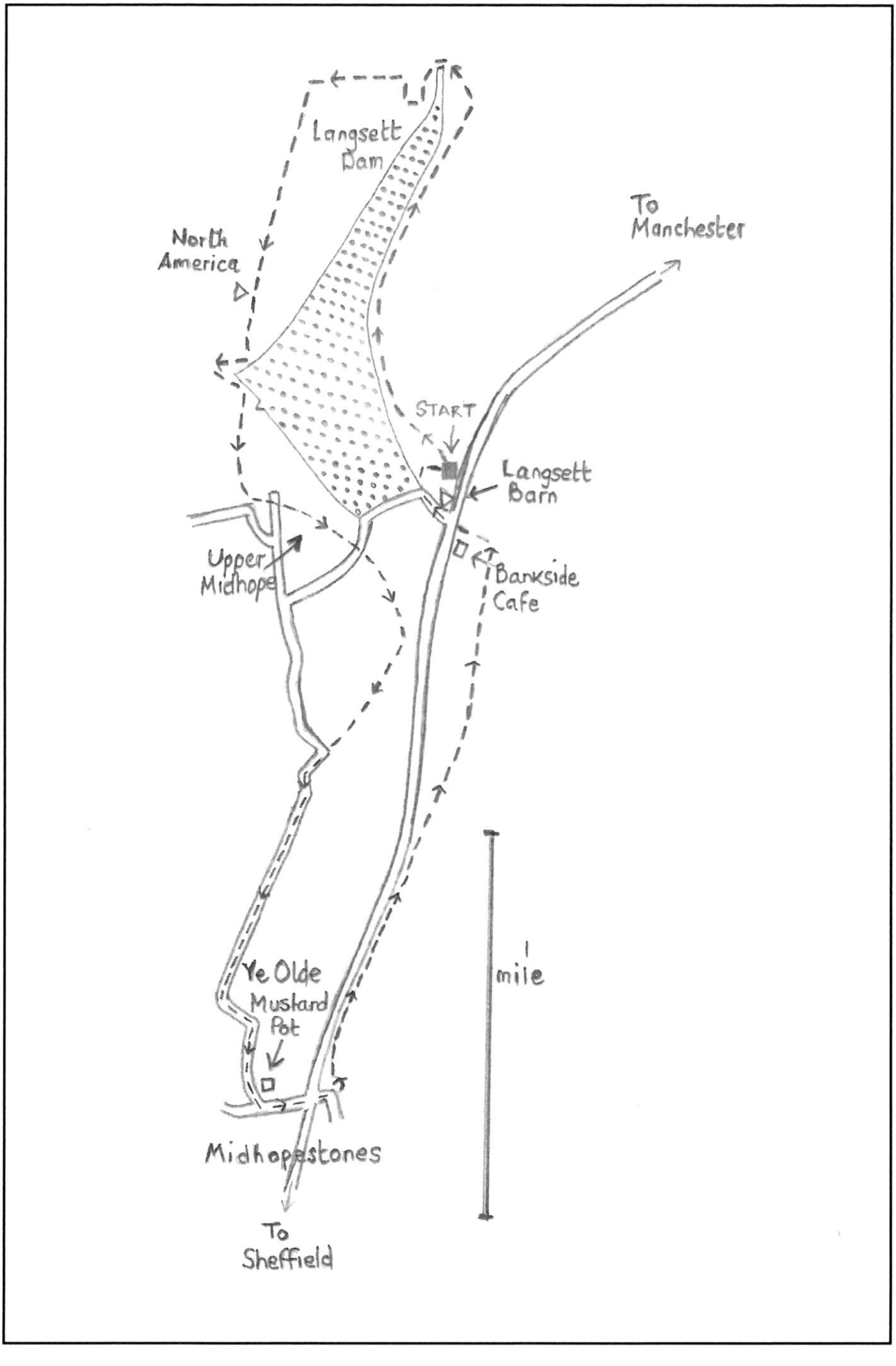
Langsett
Dam
To
Manchester
North
America
START
Langsett
Barn
Upper
Midhope
Bankside
Cafe
1
mile
Ye Olde
Mustard
Pot
Midhopestones
To
Sheffield

Walk Difficulty

There is quite a long climb at the start of the walk and for a great part of the walk the paths are rocky and uneven. Some of the field paths can get very muddy, as can the old railway path on the way back too. There are also a few tricky wall stiles to tackle.

Starting Point

The walk starts at Langsett Barn Car Park, A616, Langsett, Sheffield S36 9FD.

The Route

From the car park take a path in the corner which leads down to the reservoir. Walk alongside the reservoir to where it ends then turn left to cross the river. Carry on uphill for half a mile ignoring a minor path left to reach a junction of paths at a signpost. Go left and with the dam to the left, pass North America farm ruins to keep roughly in the same direction to reach a river which feeds the reservoir.

Here, the path becomes a track and bends right to reach a road further up. Take a path on the left which leads up a short hill to Upper Midhope. At the road go left, then after a few yards take a path right which leads down to the main road. Cross the road to enter into a field. With a wall on the right to start with the path heads towards and over a stile into woods. With the river on the left the path reaches a bridge. Ignoring the bridge crossing, go right on to a path which becomes a track and eventually reaches Midhope Hall Lane.

Go left along the lane for about a mile as it becomes Chapel Lane further on and then reaches Mortimer Road. Go left past the Olde Mustard Pot pub, and then further on cross the A616. Go under the bridge then take a track on the left and then after a few yards a path left on to the old railway line. Stay on this path for 1.5 miles as it goes through woods to start with, then in open land crosses paths, a drive and a track, keeping roughly the same distance from the main road on the left.

Bank café can be seen on the left from a long way off, and the path we need goes to the left of the café, leading out on to the road. Cross over the road to take the road opposite, then round the bend take a path right which leads back into the car park.

Look out for…..

Langsett Barn which was built in 1621 and is used as a community room.

North America farm ruins. Around the turn of the 19c it became fashionable in the UK for people to give places and buildings 'exotic-sounding' names that were being learned about from people returning from the fast-growing USA. This is how North America farm got its name. A further American link is that Canadian troops used the ruined farm for shell practice during WW2.

Dog Suitability

The walk isn't great for having dogs off lead as there are sheep and grouse on the moors, and there is some road walking too. The wooded section round Langsett Dam is fine, and the old railway part on the way back is ok too.

Refreshments

There are 2 pubs, the Olde Mustard Pot at Midhopestones, and the Waggon and Horses at Langsett. There is also Bank Café at Langsett.

Ruins of the North America farmstead at Langsett Dam

Walk No: 8 Millhouses

4.5 miles / 2-2.25 hours

Introduction

This is a lovely walk in the suburbs of Sheffield with a real mixture of surroundings, with 2 parks, three woods and 2 golf courses included. Starting with a stroll through Millhouses Park the route carries on through Hutcliffe Wood before moving on to Beauchief and the Abbey and Hall there. Then it's Ladies Spring Wood and Ecclesall Woods back to the start. This a fairly easy walk and will be suitable for anyone who is capable of walking 4-5 miles. There is a fair amount of history throughout the walk too.

Beauchief Abbey

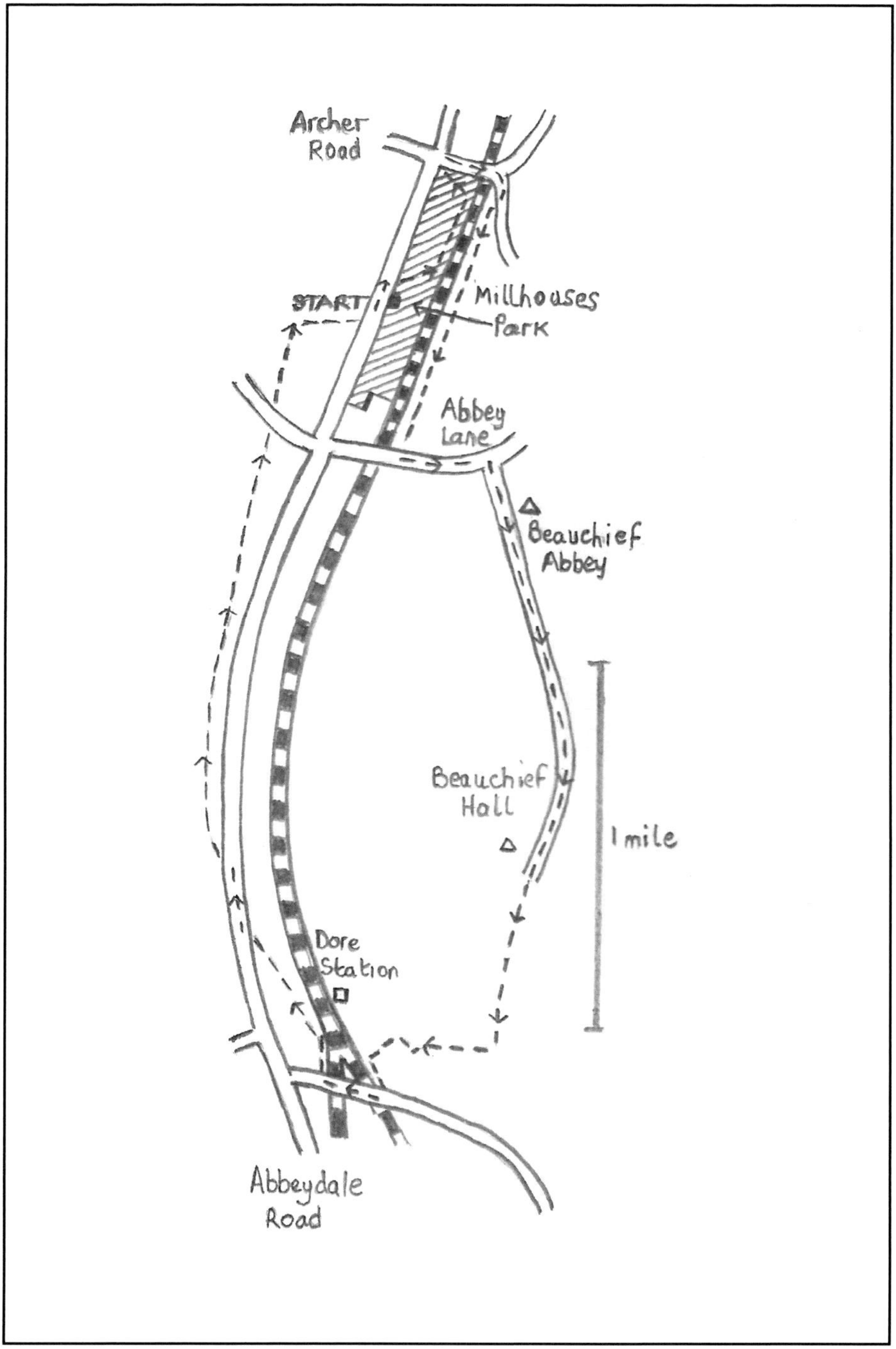
Archer Road
START
Millhouses Park
Abbey Lane
Beauchief Abbey
Beauchief Hall
1 mile
Dore Station
Abbeydale Road

Walk Difficulty

With no stiles to climb, and just a gentle climb up from Abbey Lane to Beauchief Hall this makes this a fairly easy walk. As usual, there can be mud in the woods, and the only really difficult section to watch out for is an awkward banking down through Ladies Spring Wood.

Starting Point

The route starts from Millhouses Park Café, Abbeydale Rd South, S7 2QQ

The Route

From outside the café head down to the river and follow the path towards the city centre. On reaching the road bridge, climb the steps to cross over the bridge. Walk alongside the road, then as it bends left, turn right to walk alongside Hutcliffe Wood Road for about 100 yards to enter the woods on a path on the right. This path stays level for 0.75 mile through Hutcliffe Wood, with the railway down below before emerging on to Abbey Lane.

Turn left to walk along Abbey Lane for a short distance, crossing over to reach Beauchief Abbey Lane on the right. Turn into the lane and follow it for half a mile to reach Beauchief Hall entrance gate. Turn left, then after 10 yards take an enclosed path right through hedges which after about ¼ mile ends at a golf fairway. Ignore the path right and cross the fairway through a line of trees in the direction of houses.

When the path reaches the golf club driveway turn right to head towards the clubhouse. As the drive widens to become a car park, take a path left to enter Ladies Spring Wood. The path soon bends right, then after about 75 yards, take a path left, which is soon joined by a path coming from the right. Go down the steps to the bottom, then turn left to come out on to Twentywell Lane. Turn right, and once over the bridge go right through a wooden gate on to a path which leads to Dore Station.

Through the station car park, cross the road and enter Ecclesall Woods on the third path. After a few yards at a path junction turn right to walk through the woods very soon behind houses on the right. Come out on to Abbey Lane and cross over the road to enter woods again keeping in the same direction behind houses to start with. Take either of the next two paths right down to Abbeydale Road, then cross over to enter Millhouses Park. Turn left to return to the start.

Look out for…..

Millhouses Park is situated where Ecclesall Corn mill is recorded as having been as early as 1299, when it belonged to Beauchief Abbey. A water wheel existed on the site of the boating lake from the first half of the 17c and remained in use into the mid-nineteenth century. The land was given to the City of Sheffield in 1907 and has been a park since the 1930's.

Beauchief Abbey dates from the mid 12c and was dedicated to Saint Mary and Saint Thomas Beckett. It was said that Robert FitzRanulf who built the abbey was one of the murderers of Thomas Becket and founded the abbey to make amends for his guilt. In its time the monastery owned all the farms in the valley, and also controlled industries such as iron smelting, mineral extraction, woodland industries and mills on the river. There are medieval fishponds behind the church which were used by the monks for food.

Beauchief Hall was built in 1671 by Edward Pegge whose family had acquired the estate through marriage in 1648. The Pegge family sold the house in 1923 and it became De La Salle school until 2010 when it was sold to a property development company.

Dog Suitability

Dogs will be able to be off lead on a lot of this walk through the parks and woods and there's only one small stile too.

Refreshments

Millhouses Park café and the Waggon Horses pub are both at the start of the walk on Abbeydale Road.

Walk No: 9 Loxley Valley

7.5 miles / 4 hours

Introduction

An outstanding feature of this walk are the views from 'up top', which in this case means from the ridge approaching Holdworth from Wadsley Common. With views across the valley to Dungworth, Bradfield and towards Malin Bridge this is a good way to check out life in this lovely part of Sheffield. Very few people walk up there either, which makes the area all the better to visit for a walk! With a reservoir section to walk along, and a long section of the Loxley Valley to walk through with all its industrial history, this makes a good all-round walk. It's a great walk to take a picnic to as well, with there being numerous places to stop and enjoy the surroundings such as the Commons, alongside the reservoir and in the valley itself. The route for the walk is Wadsley Common, Holdworth, Dam Flask reservoir, Loxley Valley, Low Matlock, Loxley Common. There is a mixture of paths on this walk including heathland, farm tracks and field and riverside paths.

High above Loxley Valley with Dungworth in the distance

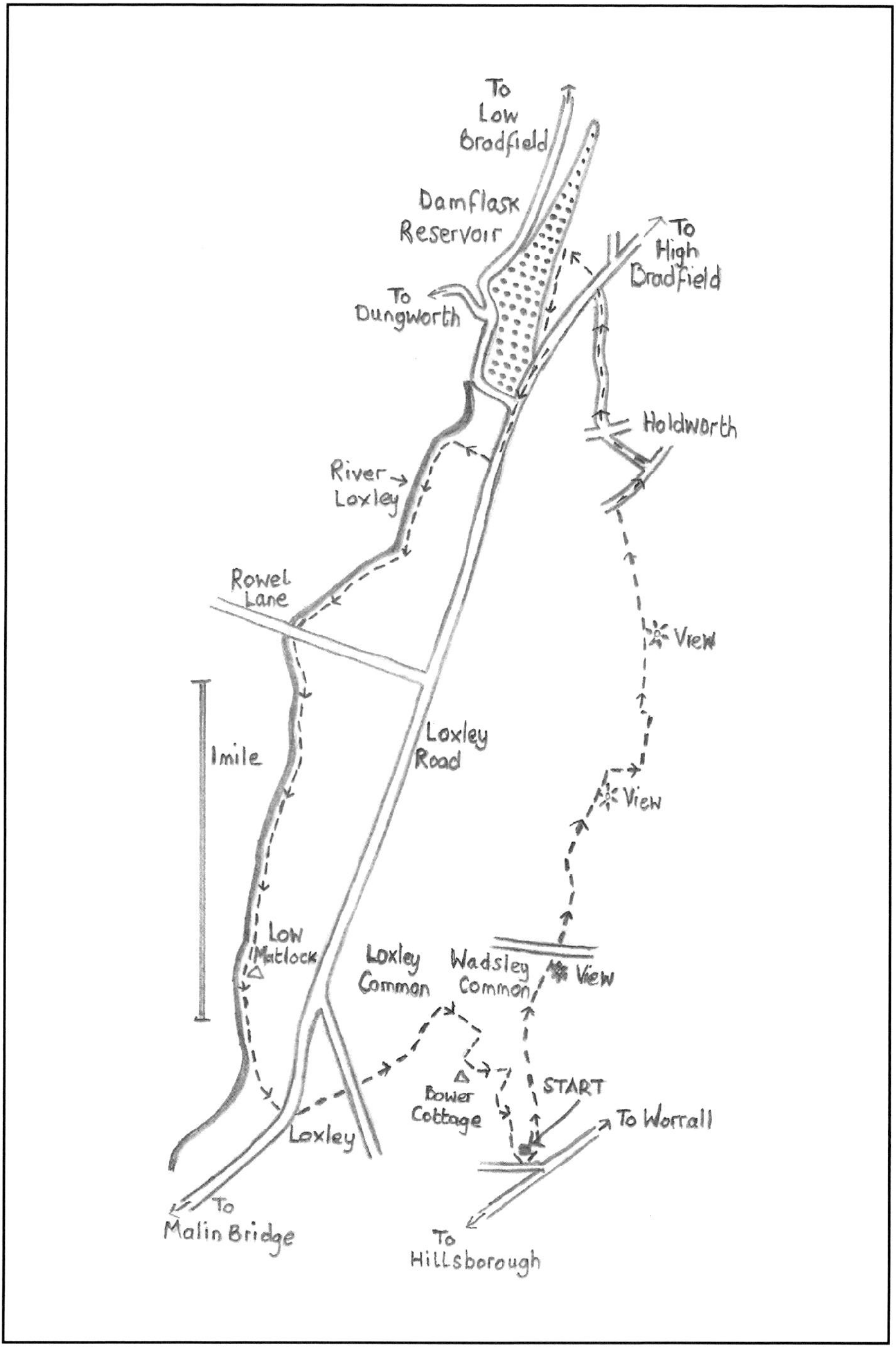
To Low Bradfield
Damflask Reservoir
To High Bradfield
To Dungworth
Holdworth
River Loxley
Rowel Lane
View
1mile
Loxley Road
View
Low Matlock
Loxley Common
Wadsley Common
View
Bower Cottage
START
To Worrall
Loxley
To Malin Bridge
To Hillsborough

Walk Difficulty

There is a lot of this walk which could be muddy in winter or after rain, especially on the path through the valley. There is just one small hill on the outward stretch, and then a longish one near the end, neither of which should be difficult for people who regularly walk up to 8 miles. Overall, the paths aren't too difficult however there are one or two tricky stiles.

Starting Point

Rural Lane Car Park, Wadsley, Sheffield, S6 4BZ

The Route

From the entrance to the car park take the path right, then after 40 yards take either path at a fork. When they join back up carry on uphill with a broken wall on the left. 30 yards after the path leaves the wall, in a small clearing take a path left which crosses a broken wall to reach a main path. Go straight across and up steps to bear right through trees. Further on at a meeting of paths, go straight on to go through a car park and on to a road.

Cross the road to a path opposite, then after a few yards at the fork, take either path, they join up further on. A few yards after the paths have joined back up take a path to the right which leads uphill into trees and eventually reaches a wall. The path goes right here and carries on uphill with the wall on the left to reach a road. Take a farm track then at a footpath sign go left, well before the farm. After a few yards go right on a path which keeps in the same direction through fields and above a house, in the direction of Holdworth.

At the road in Holdworth turn right, then take Stony Lane left. At crossroads go straight forward on to Dalroyd Lane and stay on it until it reaches Loxley Road. Go left for a few yards to take a stile on the right into a field. Follow the path signs as the path heads towards woods, but as a wall comes up in front turn right uphill to go through a gap in the wall at the top of the field.

Go half left now towards the far corner of the field to a stile into woods which leads down to Damflask reservoir. Turn left along the path to eventually come out on to Loxley Road. Turn right and stay on the road for half a mile before turning right to go down Stacey Bank.

At the bottom turn left and stay on a path close to the river until after ¼ of a mile it reaches an industrial estate road. Go left for about 200 yards then as the road bends left take a path right which re-joins the river. After another ¼ of a mile the path reaches another estate road. Turn left along it for about 100 yards then at a left bend in the road take the path right leading back to the river again. After a few minutes at Rowel Lane turn left and cross over to carry on through the valley with the river now on the right.

After 0.4 miles at cottages on the left the path joins a lane to keep in the same direction. After a couple of minutes, as the lane bends left, take a lane right which leads to the hamlet of Low Matlock. Stay on Low Matlock Lane until it comes out on to Loxley Road. Cross over to take a path to the left. At a small bridge take the path left to go through trees to reach Studfield Hill. Cross over and head half left towards houses and stay to the right of the houses as the path goes through a grassed area to reach Rodney Hill.

Take a path opposite to the right which soon leads to a junction of paths and a short track which must be taken to the right. At a lane, go left up the hill to Bower Cottage. Take a path to the right of the cottage drive gates and carry on upwards taking a fork right after a couple of minutes. At the top of the hill the path reaches a wall at the corner of a field. Carry on to the right with the wall and the field right to reach the corner of the field. Turn right then go immediate left at a Water Authority sign. Shortly. where the track goes right take a path straight on into the woods. Where the path meets other paths turn right to go back to the car park.

Look out for…..

Wadsley Common has been wooded since 1600 when its wood would have not only been used to build and furnish the primitive local cottages, but for cooking and heating as well. Trees were later used to produce poles for fencing, pit props for mining, and tool handles for the steel trade. Early records also record that in 1730 local people were charged 1 penny to go rabbiting on Wadsley Common. Dog fighting, cock fighting and even bear baiting also took place there and it is also reputed that Mary Queen of Scots exercised on horseback in the area whilst a prisoner of the Earl of Shrewsbury in Sheffield Castle.

Damflask village was washed away in the Great Sheffield Flood In 1864 when 240 people and 693 animals drowned as a result of the collapse of the Dale Dyke Dam upstream. The village stood near the site of the current dam wall and had a pub, corn mill, paper mill, wire mill, blacksmith's shop and a few houses. The village was never rebuilt after the flood because plans were already in hand to build Damflask Reservoir, which was completed in 1896.

Loxley Valley Industry came to the Loxley area in the middle of the 17th century when the first mills were set up on the River Loxley as small pocket businesses. Steel and iron forging and rolling mills were later established by the river. Many of the mill ponds associated with these mills are still present on the river and provide a haven for fish and wildlife.

Loxley Common is the supposed birthplace of Robin Hood. Legend has it that he was born in a cottage on a hillock called Little Haggis Croft around 1160. Another Loxley Common legend relates how a certain Frank Fearns was hung at York in 1782 for the murder of a local watchmaker, and his body was returned to the scene of the crime where it was gibbetted and hung "until his bones finally fell from their chains". Apparently, this took 14 years!

Bower Cottage is believed to have been built close to Robin Hood's Bower and Moss, in other words his shelter and a woodland named after him.

Dog Suitability

There is some road walking, and a couple of fields where there might be animals, but apart from that it's a great walk for dogs as they'll be able to be off lead most of the way. There are just a few difficult stiles to watch out for.

Refreshments

Close to the start/finish there's the Rose and Crown pub at Wadsley. At the top of Stacey Bank there's the Nags Head pub and at Loxley there is The Wisewood Inn, The Admiral Rodney and Loxley Post Office.

Walk No: 10 Padley Gorge

4 miles / 2.5 hours

Introduction

Padley Gorge is such an iconic place to walk, and this really interesting walk includes the entire length of the gorge from Grindleford Station all the way up to Upper Burbage Bridge. There are some delightful paths through the Longshaw Estate at the start of the walk too as the route passes Longshaw Lodge on its way down to Upper Padley. A track through the village then leads past Padley Mill to reach Padley Chapel and the ruins of Padley Manor. Following a look at the ruins a path behind the chapel enters woodland and leads to a path which goes above Padley Gorge, with the Burbage Brook crashing down below. At the top of the gorge there is a lovely clearing next to Burbage Brook popular with families and ideal for a picnic, especially as there is usually an ice cream van up there! Although the walk is only 4 miles long, there are some challenges, but it should be suitable for most abilities.

Path through Padley Gorge

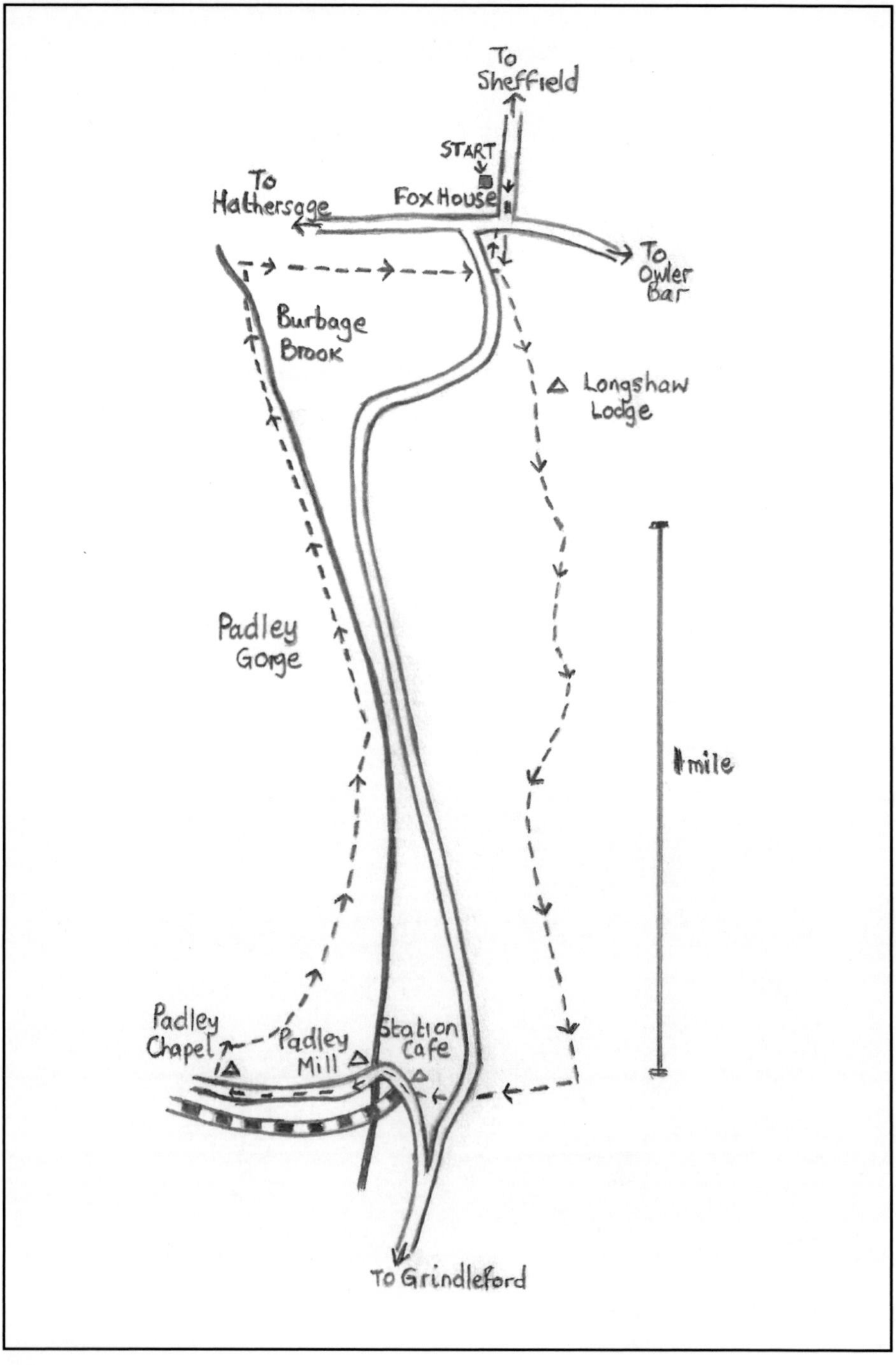
To Sheffield
START
To Hathersage
Fox House
To Owler Bar
Burbage Brook
Longshaw Lodge
1 mile
Padley Gorge
Padley Chapel
Padley Mill
Station Cafe
To Grindleford

Walk Difficulty

There is a tricky downhill section coming down from the Longshaw Estate to the station, and the climb up above Padley Gorge is strenuous but worth the effort for the views along the way. The path both through the gorge and also alongside Burbage Brook is quite rocky, and care must be taken both because of how uneven it is, but also because of the mud that is often on this section.

Starting Point

The walk starts at the Fox House pub, Hathersage Rd, Sheffield S11 7TY. There is a public car park next to the pub, or parking on Hathersage Road.

The Route

Cross the road at the junction to go through a gate and on to a path which leads down to the Longshaw Estate. At the estate road, turn left and just before reaching the Lodge look for a path down a few steps on the right. This path leads towards woods and enters the woods at a gate. Go through the gate and turn right. Go through 2 more gates, then after ¼ mile alongside a pond, go through a gate left to turn left on to a path signposted Yarncliffe.

After a few minutes, the path joins a stone covered track which joins from the right. After crossing a small stone bridge go straight forward, then after 30 yards fork right on to another grass track to reach a gate by a wall. Go through the gate and keep on this path which stays close to the wall. After 350 yards take a fork right which leads through trees down to the road.

Turn left on the road for a few yards then cross the road and turn right on to a path which leads down to Grindleford station. Pass the station and cross the bridge on this unmade track which after passing Padley Mill on the right carries on to Padley Chapel and Manor. After visiting the Manor ruins carry on in the same direction, crossing a cattle grid before turning immediate right to go uphill with a wall on the right. The path turns right alongside the wall and skirts houses before heading diagonally through trees to reach the main path through Padley Gorge. Turn left on to this path which passes above the Gorge before at the top passing through a gate to exit the woods.

Now in a clearing, keep in the same direction close to the river, quickly passing 2 wooden bridges. Half a mile further on cross a 3rd bridge on the right on to a stony path uphill which soon reaches a 'T' junction of paths. Go right here and stay on this path keeping in the same direction to reach a road. Opposite is the entranceway to the Longshaw Estate. Cross the road onto the estate road then immediately turn left on to the path back to the Fox House which was used at the start of the walk.

Look out for…..

Longshaw Estate including Longshaw Lodge was once the Duke of Rutland's shooting estate but was purchased from the Duke by public subscription in 1927 and presented to the National Trust. The estate is best well known for the sheepdog trials which are held here every September.

Totley tunnel is 3.5 miles long and took 11 years to build. Because of the damp conditions, there were outbreaks of typhoid, diphtheria, smallpox, and scarlet fever amongst the workforce, not helped by the fact that accommodation was scarce, with the workers often living thirty to a house. Working 24-hour shifts, as soon as one man got out of his bed, another would take his place, with little in the way of washing or sanitary facilities.

Padley Mill was built in 18c and served as a corn mill, sawmill and wire-drawing mill until becoming derelict in the early 1900's. It was subsequently renovated and in the 1930's became a café for a short while, serving walkers. It is now a Grade ll listed building and has been converted into a residence.

Padley Chapel is the remains of Padley Manor, built in 14c and 15c. In 1588 two Catholic priests, Robert Ludlam and Nicholas Garlick were taken from the house and hung, drawn and quartered and their remains stuck on poles in Derby city centre. Their crime was to be Catholics and not Protestants.

Dog Suitability

Dogs need to be led throughout the Longshaw Estate as there are sheep in the fields all year round. Dogs can be safely off lead though in the wooded sections. There are no stiles on this walk.

Refreshments

Refreshments can be obtained from the Fox House, a cafe at Longshaw Lodge and Grindleford café which has a great reputation.

Walk No: 11 Lodge Moor

5 miles / 2.25 hours

Introduction

This fairly easy walk on the outskirts of Sheffield straddles the Peak district National Park border and offers walkers a number of features to enjoy. Starting at the top of Wyming Brook Nature Reserve, for about a mile the first part of the walk goes high up above the Rivelin Valley through the Fox Hagg Nature Reserve, with lovely views of the dams down below. After cutting through the Hallamshire Golf Course to Lodge Moor the return section follows the Redmires Conduit to the lower Redmires Reservoir and past the reservoir houses back to the start. There are various viewpoints in the first half of the walk and loads of historical points of interest in the second section to learn about.

Rivelin Dams with Rod Moor in the background

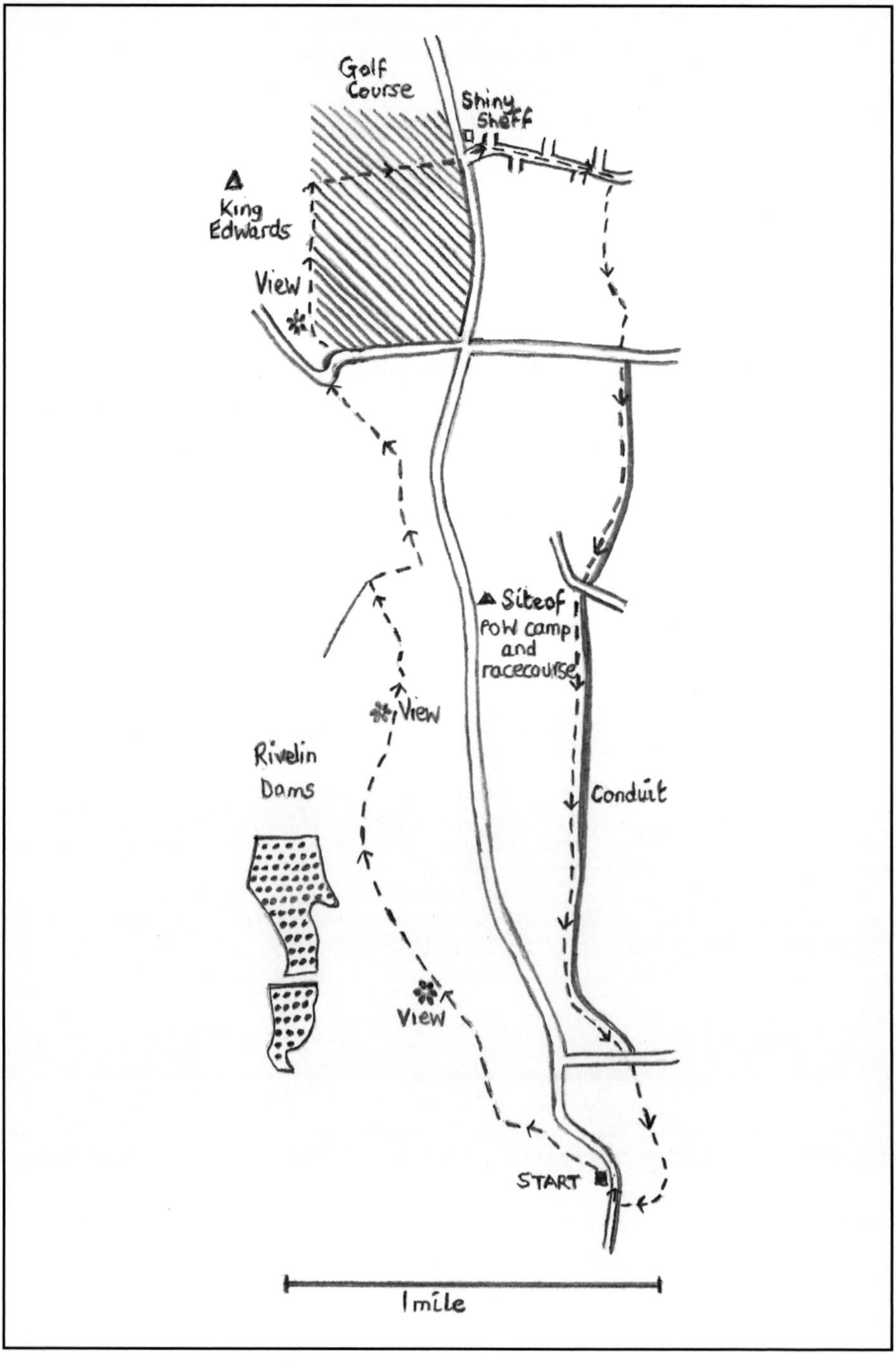
Golf Course
Shiny Sheff
King Edwards
View
Siteof POW camp and racecourse
View
Rivelin Dams
Conduit
View
START
1mile

Walk Difficulty

At the start of the walk there are steppingstones over Wyming Brook which some people might prefer not to cross, in which case there is a diversion which may be taken along the road. The path through Fox Hagg is very undulating and care must be taken with tree roots and overhanging branches on this section. There are also steep drops alongside the path in places, and a particularly tricky banking to get down to cross a stream too. There is just one stile on the walk, and no farm animals anywhere on the route.

Starting Point

Wyming Nature Reserve Car Park, Redmires Road, S10 4QX. The postcode for the car park may cover a wide area in which case an easier way to find the start point is to find The Three Merry Lads pub, Redmires Rd, Sheffield S10 4LJ, and the car park is ¾ of a mile past the pub on the same side of the road.

The Route

There are 2 choices from the car park. The first is to take the steps down to the river and cross it via the steppingstones, then at a path crossroads on the other side of the river take the path signposted Fox Hagg to go up a banking. After a few yards branch left to take the path along the top of the valley. The alternative to avoid the steppingstones is to come out of the car park on to the road and turn left, and then after 100 yards take a path left up a small banking. After 40 yards take the path right, which is the one mentioned earlier which runs along the top of the valley. Stay on this path for exactly a mile until approaching a wall corner on the right a path joins it from the left.

This path leads round the corner of the wall above a small ravine on the left for a short while until it reaches a path on the left which drops down to cross a stream. The path turns left here to go along the other side of the ravine. Keep on this path ignoring a path to the right until you reach a road. Turn right to go uphill for about 30 yards, then take the footpath sign on the left.

The path here bends right with a golf course on the other side of a wall. There is a fantastic viewing point next to two benches on the left here. Back to the route, where the wall ends bear right to go down a steep banking to cross a stream before climbing the banking on the other side. After a few minutes take some steps on the right which lead to a gap in a wall leading to the golf course. This path cuts straight across a fairway to come out on to Redmires Road opposite the Shiny Sheff pub.

Cross Redmires Road and walk along the right side of Crimicar Lane. After crossing 2 roads, take a footpath on the right which initially skirts a cricket pitch and then goes through playing fields to come out on to a road. Cross this road to walk alongside Redmires Conduit to cross a second road. Stay on the path with the Conduit on one side and a park and playing fields on the other side to start with, and then further on a plantation. Eventually the path comes out on to Soughley Road.

The conduit goes underground here as the route continues by crossing the road on to a path which keeps in the same direction to enter a wood. After going over 2 stone stiles the path joins a path coming from the left to go downhill to reach an ex-Water Authority service road. Turn right on to the road which goes between houses to reach Redmires Road. Turn right here and the car park is a few yards further down the road on the right.

Look out for…..

Rivelin Dams. The Rivelin Dams are part of a series of reservoirs built to the west of the city known as Sheffield Lakeland and were built in the 1840's.

The King Edward VII Orthopaedic Hospital in the Rivelin Valley owed its existence to the fondness that the people of Sheffield had for King Edward VII who died in 1910. On his death a fund was set up and the population of the City raised £18,000 in his memory with the organisers arranging for the money to be used to build a hospital school for disabled children. The hospital is now a residential development.

The Redmires Conduit was built in the 1830s to supply water to Sheffield prior to the Redmires reservoirs being built for this reason. The conduit taps the source of the River Rivelin out on the moors, and after bending round the side of the Redmires dams it runs past the old POW camp area, and the back of the old Lodge Moor hospital and on to Blackbrook Road where it goes underground.

Redmires POW camp was situated in the plantation which is located just past the Sportsman Inn. There were 2 camps from both world wars with the WW1 camp being the largest, covering most of the woods. Among WW1 prisoners was Admiral Karl Doenitz, head of the German navy and the man who took over the Third Reich after Adolf Hitler committed suicide.

Redmires Racecourse was built in 1875 opposite the Three Merry Lads, also where the plantation now is, and where the POW camps were built. The racecourse consisted of 65 acres and the race meetings usually lasted 3 days. As there were no motor vehicles at this time to bring the horses in horseboxes, they were brought to Sheffield in train carriages, and then walked up to Lodge Moor. The course was elaborately laid out and enclosed, and included a grandstand. The horses and jockeys were accommodated in Racecourse Farm, (since demolished) with the jockeys being housed above the horse boxes. The course was abandoned after two or three years because of poor attendances, probably due to its remote location.

Dog Suitability

This is a great walk for having your dog off lead with there being no farm animals on any of the paths, and there being just a small amount of road walking.

Refreshments

The 3 pubs on Redmires Road in Lodge Moor are the Three Merry Lads, the Shiny Sheff, and the Sportsman. There are also shops selling drinks and snacks on Rochester Road in Lodge Moor.

Walk No: 12 Norfolk Heritage Trail

4.5 miles / 2.5 hours

Introduction

The official Norfolk Heritage Trail is a 3-mile linear route which starts at Manor Lodge and finishes at the Cathedral. To make this into a round walk, the route for this book misses out the Cathedral, the Old Queens Head and Park Hill from the 'official' map and includes Sheffield Amphitheatre and Skye Edge instead. The trail takes its name from the Dukes of Norfolk and showcases a lot of the history of Sheffield. As well as the Tudor Manor Lodge, there's also an ancient woodland, the rolling green space of one of the country's oldest public parks, and memorials and monuments which serve as reminders of the epidemics and wars that have afflicted Sheffield over the centuries. There are also Victorian almshouses in the middle of some grand Victorian houses. The route is almost entirely on tarmacked paths and there is just one short, sharp climb up Norfolk Park which is well worth the effort for the views of the city from up there.

A view of the city from Norfolk Park

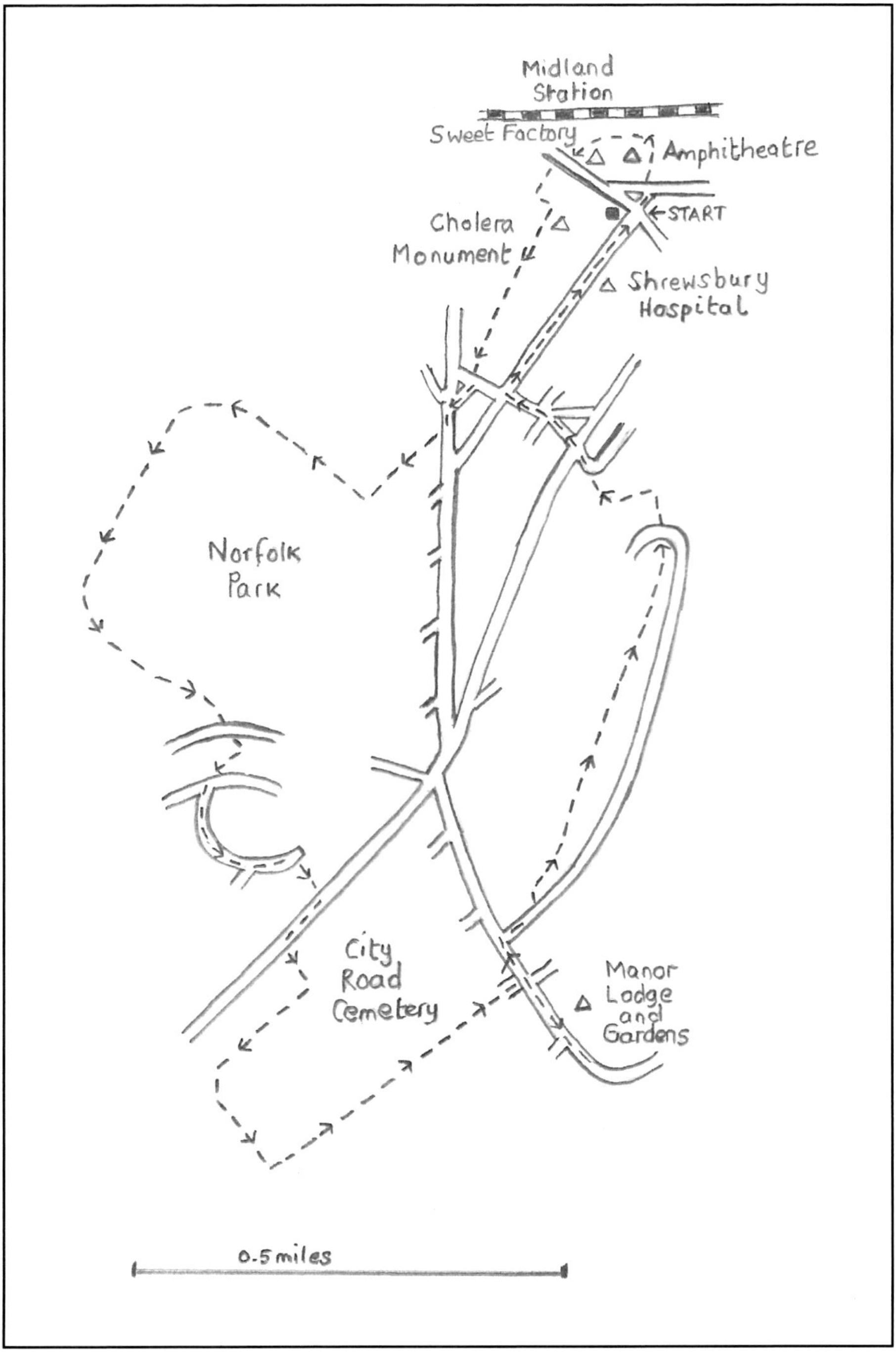
Midland Station
Sweet Factory
Amphitheatre
START
Cholera Monument
Shrewsbury Hospital
Norfolk Park
City Road Cemetery
Manor Lodge and Gardens
0.5 miles

Walk Difficulty

Just the one steep hill from the bottom to the top of Norfolk Park makes this an easy walk.

Starting Point

To take advantage of the fact that there is free on-street parking on Norfolk Road this is where the walk route starts; but it could also be started from anywhere on the walk. The postcode for Norfolk Road is S2 2ST.

The Route

Starting from the junction of Shrewsbury Road and Norfolk Road, head towards the Midland Station by going down the steep steps at the side of the amphitheatre. At the bottom of the steps turn left to walk below the amphitheatre and keep on this path to reach Granville Road. Cross the road and take a path slightly right to go up Clay Wood Bank and into the Cholera Monument Grounds. From the monument take the path on the right leading into the woods and keep on this path to cross over Fitzwalter Road on to Claywood Road to reach Granville Road at the end of the road.

Turn left to go uphill to the crossing then cross Granville Road to enter Norfolk Park. After 200 yards take the right fork and stay on this park road as it soon bends left to go uphill. At the top, stay on the road as it starts to go downhill. After it passes playgrounds on both sides, take a path right into trees which leads to steps on to St Aidan's Avenue. Turn left, and just before the road junction take a path right to cross St Aidan's Road.

A path opposite zig zags uphill and comes out on to St Aidan's Drive. Turn left, then immediate right to St Aidan's Rise and cross to the left side as the road as it bends round to reach a gennel in the far corner. Go through the gennel to reach City Road then turn right and cross the road to enter the cemetery. After a walk round the graves, head for the exit situated halfway down the left-hand side which leads on to Harwich Street. At the end of the road go right to walk along Manor Lane to reach Manor Lodge.

Just past the lodge and through the lodge car park are some lovely gardens which are worth a visit, as well as the Rhubarb Shed café. After viewing the gardens turn back along Manor Lane, then after about 250 yards go right on to Skye Edge Avenue. Just after the medical centre go left on to a grass path parallel to the road and stay on it until it reaches a road. Cross the road to take a path opposite which drops down to Fitzwalter Road. At the end, cross City Road to stay on Fitzwalter Road, then cross Stafford Road staying on Fitzwalter Road to reach Norfolk Road. Go right to return to the start.

Look out for…..

Sheffield Amphitheatre opened in 2011 and since then has regularly hosted performances such as The Greatest Showman and Bohemian Rhapsody.

The Sweet Factory was originally built as an early 19c chapel or Sunday school, and was a sweet factory for most of the 20c right up to the 1970's.

The Cholera Monument was built in 1835 on land donated by the Duke of Norfolk to bury 339 of the 402 victims of the cholera epidemic 3 years earlier. The only grave that is marked is that of John Blake who was the Master Cutler. The monument is situated next to Clay Wood, an ancient woodland.

Norfolk Park was opened in 1848 and was one of the first parks in the country to be free to the general public. When Queen Victoria visited in 1897 50,00 children sang patriotic songs and hymns to her. Before this, the park was a huge deer park, as was the area surrounding it. The former gas lamp on Granville Road was built in 1867 and was previously situated on Queens Road.

City Road Cemetery is the largest cemetery in the city covering 100 acres. It is also the grandest, with its gothic-style chapels, its Grade II listed gatehouse and clock tower, and panoramic views across the city. There are also several war memorials: one commemorates the Belgian troops and refugees who died in Sheffield during the first world war, and another is dedicated to the memory of those who died in both world wars. 134 civilian victims of the Sheffield blitz of 12 and 15 December 1940 also rest in what has become known as the Blitz Garden.

Manor Lodge was built in the 16c and was originally a hunting lodge in the deer park and later became a stately home for the Lords of the Manor. Mary Queen of Scots was imprisoned there 1570-1584 while she was in the captive custody of its owners George Talbot the 6th Earl of Shrewsbury, and Bess of Hardwick, as ordered by Queen Elizabeth I.

Shrewsbury hospital was built in 1673 from money bequeathed by Gilbert Talbot the 7th Earl of Shrewsbury who died in 1616. He asked for a hospital to be built that would care for twenty of Sheffield's poorest people. The hospital (which, at that time, meant hostel or hospice, rather than infirmary) originally opened close to the current Park Square roundabout. In the 1820s it was rebuilt in the fashionable gothic style of the day on Norfolk Road.

Dog Suitability

Dogs will need to be led for most of this walk apart from a short stretch through Clay Wood, a circuit of Norfolk Park and the Skye Edge section.

Refreshments

The café at Norfolk Park Centre in the Park and the Rhubarb Shed at Manor Lodge are great places for refreshments and there is also the Manor Castle pub on Manor Lane.

Summer scene in Clay Wood

Walk No: 13 Stanage and Moscar

8.25 miles / 4.5 hours

Introduction

This is quite a tough old walk, and because of the amount of climbing and the rocky terrain it is best suited to experienced walkers. There are a variety of paths from a bit of road walking to grassy sections, rough farm tracks and moorland paths. The route starts by crossing Hallam Moors before it heads down to the Rivelin Valley. From there it passes through the Hollow Meadows area with views over the Rivelin Valley to reach Moscar Heights. From Moscar its back down to the A57 and on to part of the Sheffield Country Walk path which leads to Stanage End, and then on to the Edge itself to enjoy the fantastic views towards the Ladybower Reservoir. On the way back the route joins Long Causeway to pass Stanedge Pole to get back to Redmires. There is a total height gain on the walk of 1100 feet (330 metres).

Walking group on Stanage Edge

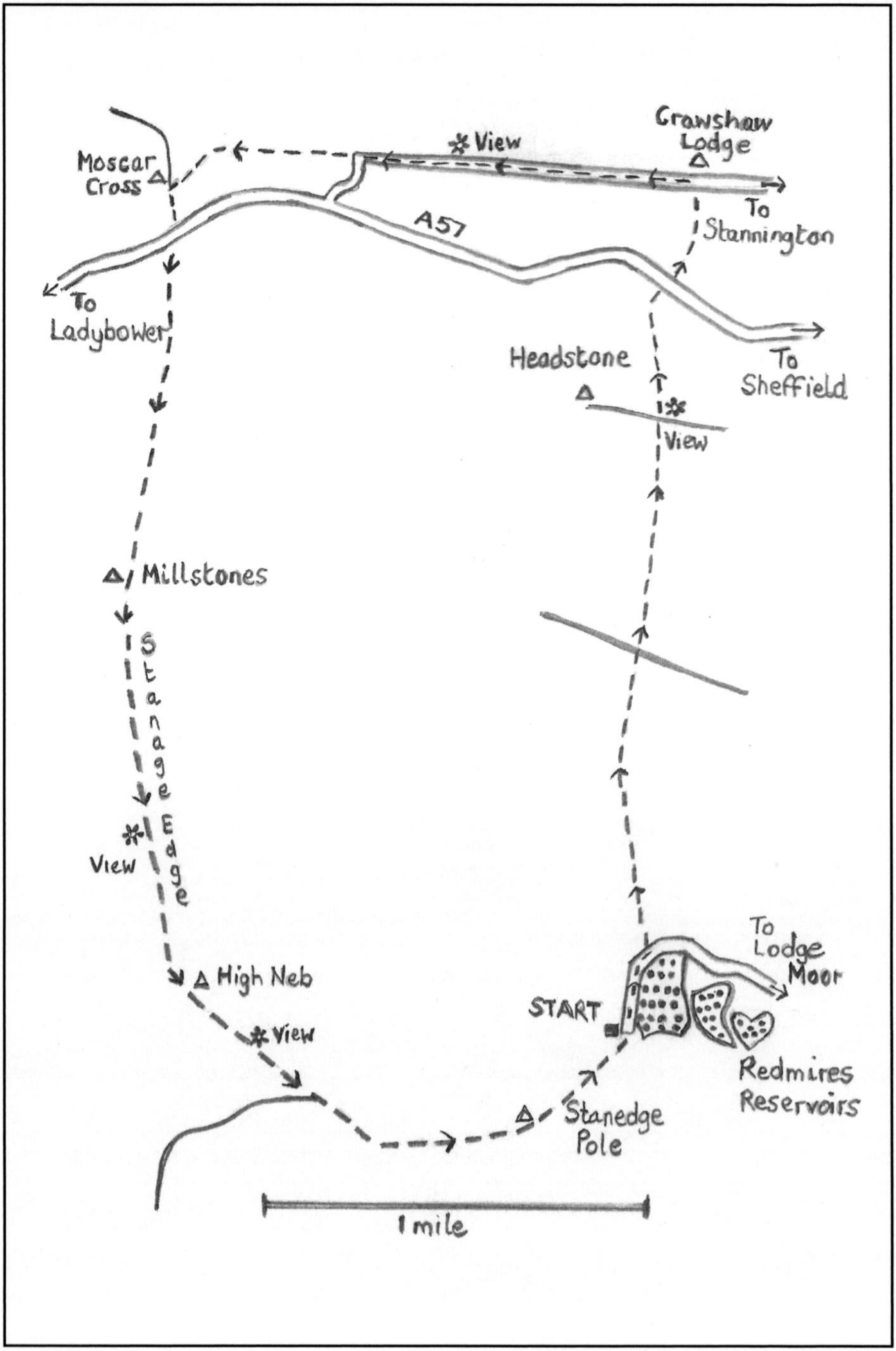
Crawshaw Lodge
View
Moscar Cross
A57
To Stannington
To Ladybower
Headstone
To Sheffield
View
Millstones
Stanage Edge
View
High Neb
View
To Lodge Moor
START
Redmires Reservoirs
Stanedge Pole
1 mile

Walk Difficulty

There is a steep climb from the Rivelin up to the road above Hollow Meadows and another climb on to Stanage, where the rocky path can also have a good deal of standing water and mud, especially after rain. There are a few tricky stiles to tackle, and Hallam Moors can be very boggy after rain too.

Starting Point

The walk starts at the end of Redmires Road alongside the Upper reservoir when coming from the Lodge Moor direction. There is usually plenty of roadside parking there. There is no postcode for the starting point however the postcode for the Three Merry Lads 2 miles away is S10 4LJ and after passing the pub on the right the starting point is at the end of that road.

The Route

Walk back along the road and where it bends right take a path left, to the right of the car park. Stay on this path for ¾ of a mile keeping in the same direction to reach a path crossing left and right. Go over a stile opposite to keep in the same direction heading downhill towards the Rivelin Valley. At a cross paths, the Headstone rock can be seen to the left. Go straight across, then at the bottom cross the bridge and ignore a path right to go over a stile into a field which leads to the A57. Cross over to a stile to the right of a gate. Continue uphill over a series of wall stiles heading towards a large house.

Turn left at the road and walk along the road for just over a mile until where it bends left a track leads straight across towards Moscar Cross Farm. After passing the farm on the left, turn left alongside a wall to return to the A57 again. After crossing the road turn right and then after a few yards take a path left and over a stile on to a path which leads to the Edge.

Continue to climb up to the Edge then at a fork bear left to stay on a path at the top of the Edge as it bends to the left. 2.75 miles after leaving the A57 a wide bridleway, Long Causeway joins the path from below on the right.

Keep on Long Causeway as the Stanage Edge path leaves it after a few yards on the right. After just over half a mile Stanedge Pole is passed on the right and Long Causeway drops down to reach the road where the walk started.

Look out for…..

The Headstone which is a large naturally occurring upright block of grit stone surrounded by a sea of smaller rocks. Due to the many fractures in the rock and viewed from the right angle it appears to have facial features.

Crawshaw Lodge. In the grounds of the lodge there is a ruined building which used to be a mausoleum. The Mausoleum contained the remains of the parents of Horatio Bright along with other family members. Horatio Bright was an eccentric Steel Merchant who died in 1907.

Moscar Cross is an old packhorse junction and a parish boundary. It is also said to be the location of 'Whitcross' in Charlotte Brontë's novel Jane Eyre.

Millstones. Many of these were abandoned when cheaper millstones started to come over from France. The French stones were harder and could grind the flour finer.

High Neb. The trigpoint here is 458 metres above sea level. 1500 feet.

Long Causeway is 2.5 miles long and was a Medieval packhorse route which ran between Sheffield and Hathersage. In the past, the route has been marked on maps as a Roman Road between Templeborough and Buxton.

Stanedge Pole is at the southernmost edge of Yorkshire. It is an ancient way marker which marks the boundary between Derbyshire and South Yorkshire. It stands at 438 metres, 1437 feet and has been there since 1550. Due to its deteriorating state it was replaced in April 2016.

Dog Suitability

Throughout a lot of the Stanage and Hallam Moors sections of the walk there are sheep dotted about, but as there aren't usually all that many of them dogs can be off lead if kept under control, as the countryside laws dictate.

Refreshments

Unfortunately, there is nowhere on the walk to obtain any refreshments. There nearest places are the pubs at Lodge Moor which are the Three Merry Lads, The Sportsman and The Shiny Sheff.

Walk No: 14 Hathersage Booths

4.5 miles / 2.25 hours

Introduction

On the outskirts of Hathersage is Hathersage Booths, a collection of houses and farms on a hill, served by a country pub. The Booths as it sometimes referred to locally is the halfway point of this lovely, fairly easy country walk in stunning countryside. Starting from Grindleford the first half of the walk leads through fields on a lovely stretch of the River Derwent, with the river on one side and the Hope Valley railway line on the other. Almost within sight of Hathersage the route then leads up a sharp hill to the turn round point at Hathersage Booths, and the possibility of a drink with a view at the Millstone Country Inn. From there, it's an old pack horse route down to Padley before crossing more fields to return to the start.

Pack Horse route from Hathersage Booths to Upper Padley

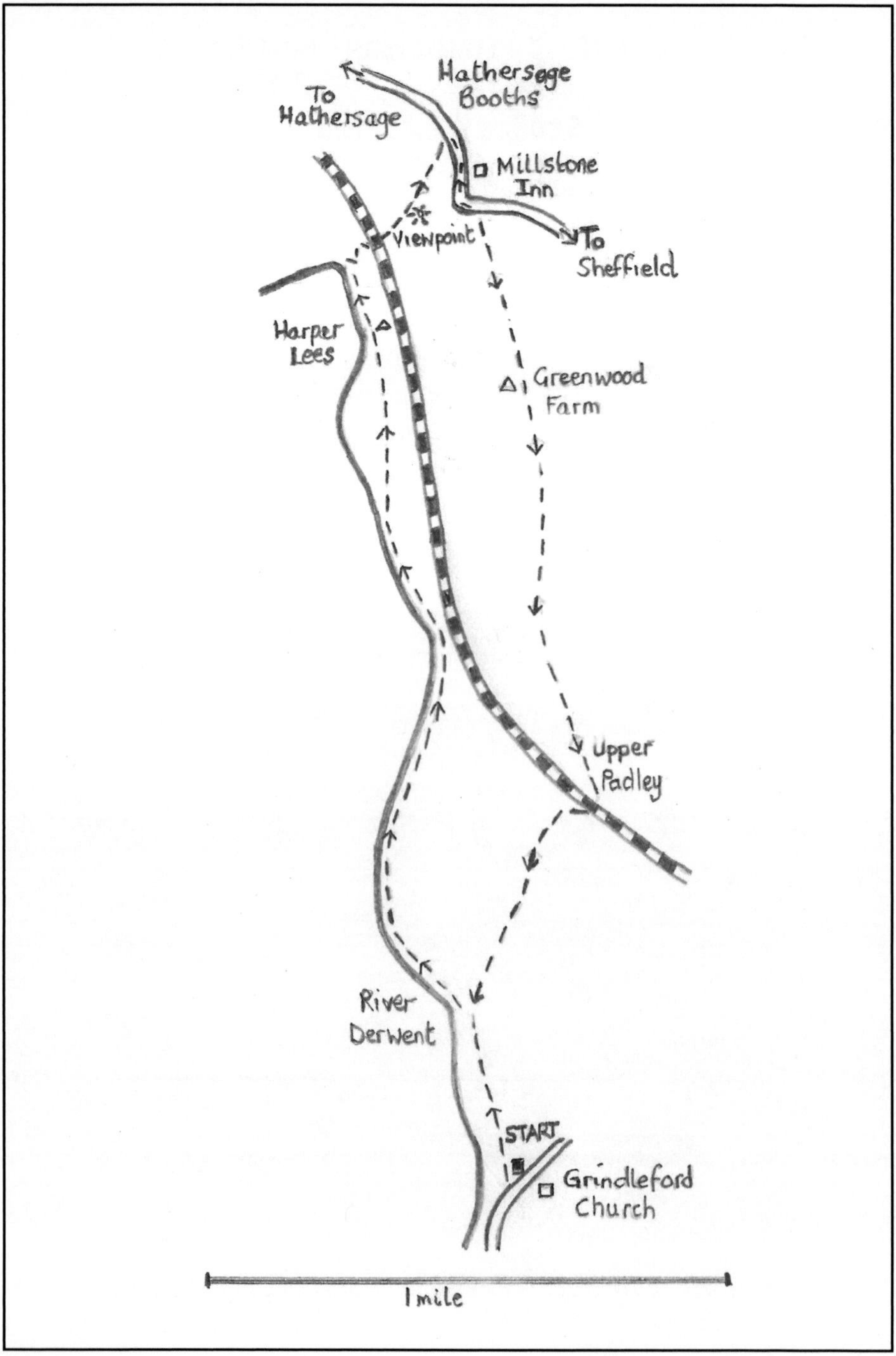
Hathersage
Booths
To
Hathersage
Millstone
Inn
Viewpoint
To
Sheffield
Harper
Lees
Greenwood
Farm
Upper
Padley
River
Derwent
START
Grindleford
Church
1 mile

Walk Difficulty

Nice and easy for the most part, with just the 15-minute hill as the only physically difficult part of the walk. Care must be taken on an unmanned railway crossing, and crossing the busy Sheffield Road at Hathersage Booths, and there could be the usual mud after rain too.

Starting Point

St Helen's church, 1 Main Rd, Grindleford, S32 2JN is the starting point for this walk where roadside parking is usually available.

The Route

Cross the road from the church and go through the squeeze stile next to a gate to enter a field alongside the river. Through this first field cross a stream, then take the left fork to keep close to the river for almost 1.25 miles to reach a large house, Harper Lees. The path here leads on to the drive for the house and carries on in the same direction for 0.25 miles. Where the drive turns sharp left, take a path on the right which bends right up a steep bank.

This path then zig zags up to the railway line which must be crossed to carry on climbing uphill with a wall on the left, heading towards houses at the top of the hill. Halfway up the hill the path goes through a gap in the wall and carries on in the same direction, with the wall now on the right. At the top of the field the path goes through a gate and into the middle of the houses. Turn left to walk a short distance to the main road.

At this point the quickest and easiest way back is to turn right along the main road, and then after 350 yards take a track on the right, at the point where the road bends left. To have a look at Hathersage Booths and/or visit the Millstone Inn though, cross over the road and take an unmade road straight opposite which leads to the right and goes between houses. Ignoring a lane down the side of the pub, keep straight on, then just after the last house on the left take a path on the right which leads back to the main road. Turn left and after a few yards cross the road to the track opposite.

The track leads downhill keeping in the same direction for just over a mile to reach Upper Padley. After passing a few houses on the right and just before the chapel, take a path right which goes over a railway bridge and into a field. A short way along this path turn left at a fingerpost to take a path through a field and rough ground to reach the stream which was crossed earlier on in the walk. Retrace steps back to the start.

Look out for…..

Harper Lees. There has been a house on this 30-acre site since 13c with the current house having been built in the 19c..

Hathersage Booths is so-called because historically, in severe weather, herdsmen would have used booths or huts for their stock, and there were a number of booths all along the road out of Hathersage. The road was even known as Booth Road before it was re-named Sheffield Road.

The Millstone Inn is an old coaching inn and having once served the workers in the nearby millstone quarries is now a favourite haunt for climbers and walkers.

Drystone wall at Greenwood Farm. A farmer who lived at the farm, along with his brother, built this wall in 1954 with the stone trough which is positioned in it being cut from neighbouring quarries. Only sheep are now kept on the farm but in 1954 cattle were kept there as well, and they are notorious for demolishing drystone walls by rubbing against them, particularly when taking water from a trough. The farmer's solution to this problem was to provide scratching posts, made from old millstones, incorporated into the wall. The hill above Greenwood Farm was known for the production of millstones, but when the market suddenly collapsed hundreds of cut stones ready for sale were abandoned on the hillside and were perfect for the farmer and his wall.

Dog Suitability

As there are usually sheep down by the river dogs must be kept under close control there, but they can be off lead on the track which leads down to Upper Padley for most of the way.

Refreshments

There is a café and shop inside Grindleford church, and there's the Millstone Country Inn at Hathersage Booths.

Unusual drystone wall at Greenwood Farm near Hathersage Booths

Walk No: 15 Redmires

4 miles / 2 hours

Introduction

This walk includes a good look at all three Redmires reservoirs from near and far, and also includes a walk through a disused quarry, and the site of a WW2 air crash. The route starts with a bit of road walking to pass all three reservoirs before passing reservoir houses and disused waterworks to a short, sharp hill which leads to the quarry. Then it's another short stretch of road walking to get to another steepish hill to reach the top of Rud Hill, and the crash site. A boggy hike through an area called White Stones gives some lovely views of the reservoirs from high up on the way back to the start.

Middle and Upper Redmires Reservoirs

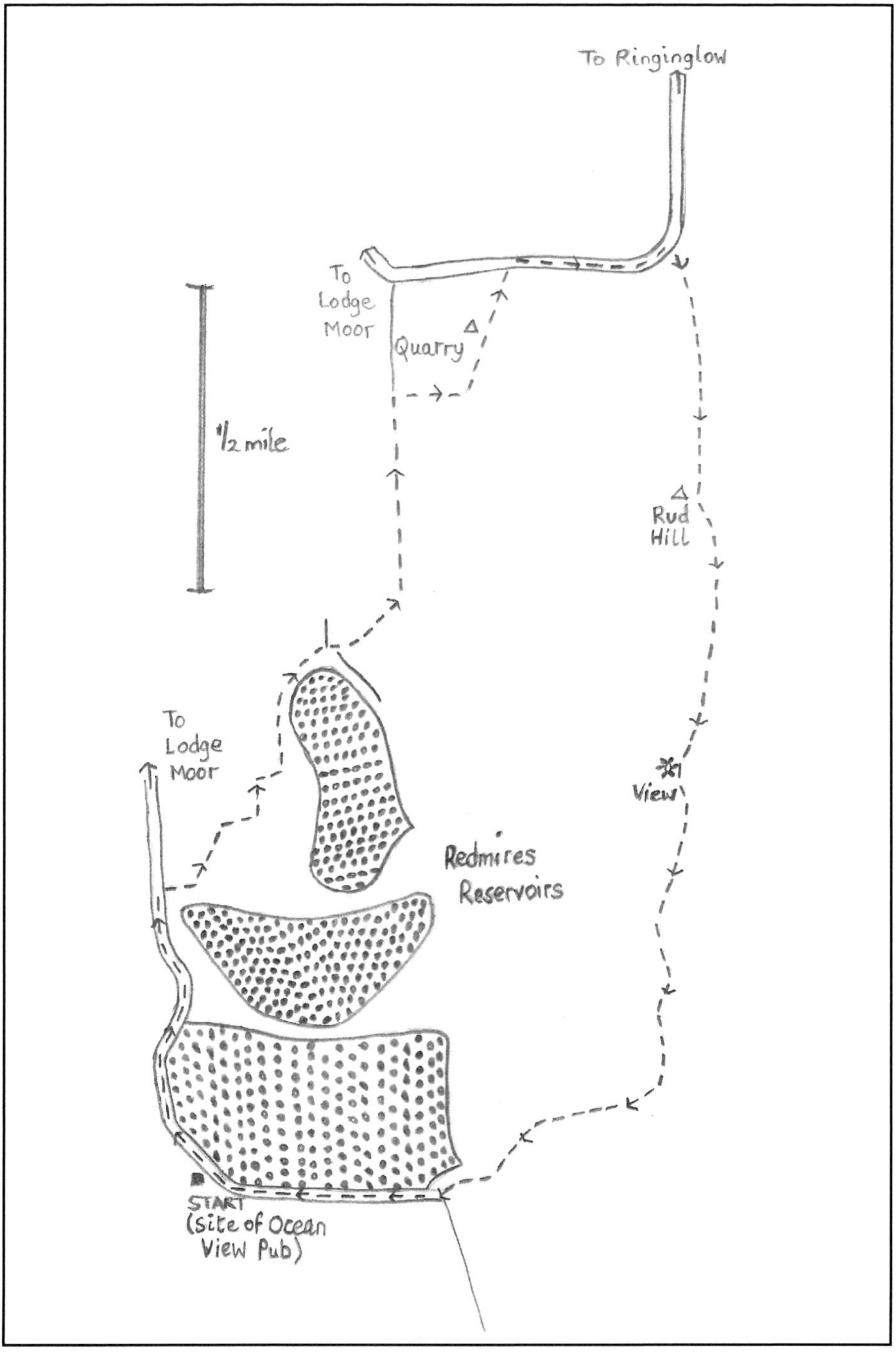
To Ringinglow
To
Lodge
Moor
Quarry
½ mile
Rud
Hill
To
Lodge
Moor
View
Redmires
Reservoirs
START
(Site of Ocean
View Pub)

Walk Difficulty

The 2 short, sharp hills on this walk aren't too difficult, however the section from Rud Hill back to the start is usually muddy, no matter what time of year. This is a walk where stout boots, or even wellies are a must!

Starting Point

The starting point for this walk is the Upper Redmires Reservoir Car Park, Long Causeway, S10 4QZ. If the car park is full, there is on-street parking close by.

The Route

Leave the car park and turn left to walk back along the road. The road starts to go downhill to pass the middle reservoir with a high bank on the right. At woods on the right go over a stile to enter the woods and stay on this path as it comes out on to a Water Authority road. Go left along the short road then turn right on to a road which passes between reservoir houses.

After about 30 yards take an enclosed path on the left through trees. After a short while the path bends right and reaches a gate. Go through the gate and ignore a path left to reach another gate. There is a path on the right here which goes round the lower reservoir but ignore this to go straight ahead to take a steep enclosed path uphill with fields on both sides.

At the top of the hill the path bends left and then after a short while there is a stile on the right which leads across a field towards farm buildings. As the path reaches a track, it turns left and heads across to Fulwood Road. Turn right to walk along the road and after about 5 minutes as the road bends left go over a ladder stile on the right and on to a track leading uphill.

A short way up the hill take the right-hand gate of two to carry on in a field uphill with a wall on the left. Go over a stile at the top of the hill and carry on in the same direction across moorland to reach another stile. The path becomes indistinct here as it winds left and right but still keeps in the same direction through a boggy area.

After about 20 minutes a clearer path leads downhill to the right, just before 2 remote trees ahead. The path now follows a line of marker posts to eventually curve round to the right towards the top corner of the upper reservoir. At a stile turn left to cross a bridge and stay on this path until it comes out on to the end of Redmires Road. Walk along the road to reach the car park at the first corner.

Look out for…..

Ocean View public house was located in the Redmires car park in 19c. Along with other pubs in the area the Ocean View was built to serve the navvies who worked on the building of the reservoirs and lived in tents and temporary homes nearby. After the reservoir building was complete, the pub struggled to attract business, and closed within a few years.

Fulwood Booth Quarry produced stone slate or thin flagstone which was used for roofing and pathing. The quarry ceased to be profitable by 1900 when the railways brought cheap Welsh slate as a lightweight substitute.

Rud Hill Air crash occurred in July 1942. An RAF Wellington on a night navigation exercise crashed into the moor at Rud Hill at half past midnight. The mostly Australian crew all survived, though suffered some injuries in the crash. A Home Guard contingent of 20 men happened to be in the area and 10 of them tramped across the moor in the rain to reach the burning wreck and pulled the crew clear of the flames while ammunition was going off all around them. The officer in charge, Sergeant Lowey received a Certificate of Gallantry for his efforts, the highest honour a Home Guard can be awarded.

Dog Suitability

There are normally sheep on the moorland section, and horses in one field that the route crosses, and with the bits of road walking this means that unfortunately this is not a walk where dogs can be off lead very much.

Refreshments

There is nowhere to obtain refreshments during the walk however there is a café at the Alpaca Farm at Ringinglow and the Norfolk Arms pub. There are also pubs and shops at Lodge Moor.

Walk No: 16 Worrall

4 miles / 2.25 hours

Introduction

This is a tough old walk in the Worrall area which has quite a few difficult obstacles and if undertaken in winter can be very muddy too. Because of this, it is more suited to experienced walkers than casual strollers. At the worst spot for mud there is an alternative for anyone who prefers mud-avoidance. Starting from the centre of Worrall the route quickly moves on to field paths and quiet country lanes whilst passing through the hamlet of Onesacre to reach the outskirts of Oughtibridge. Then it's more field paths and lanes, followed by a short visit to the lovely Coumes Wood on the way back. There are great views of the Upper Don Valley and Wharncliffe Woods and Chase on some sections of the walk, and some interesting woodland sections too.

Field at Onesacre with Wharncliffe Chase in the background

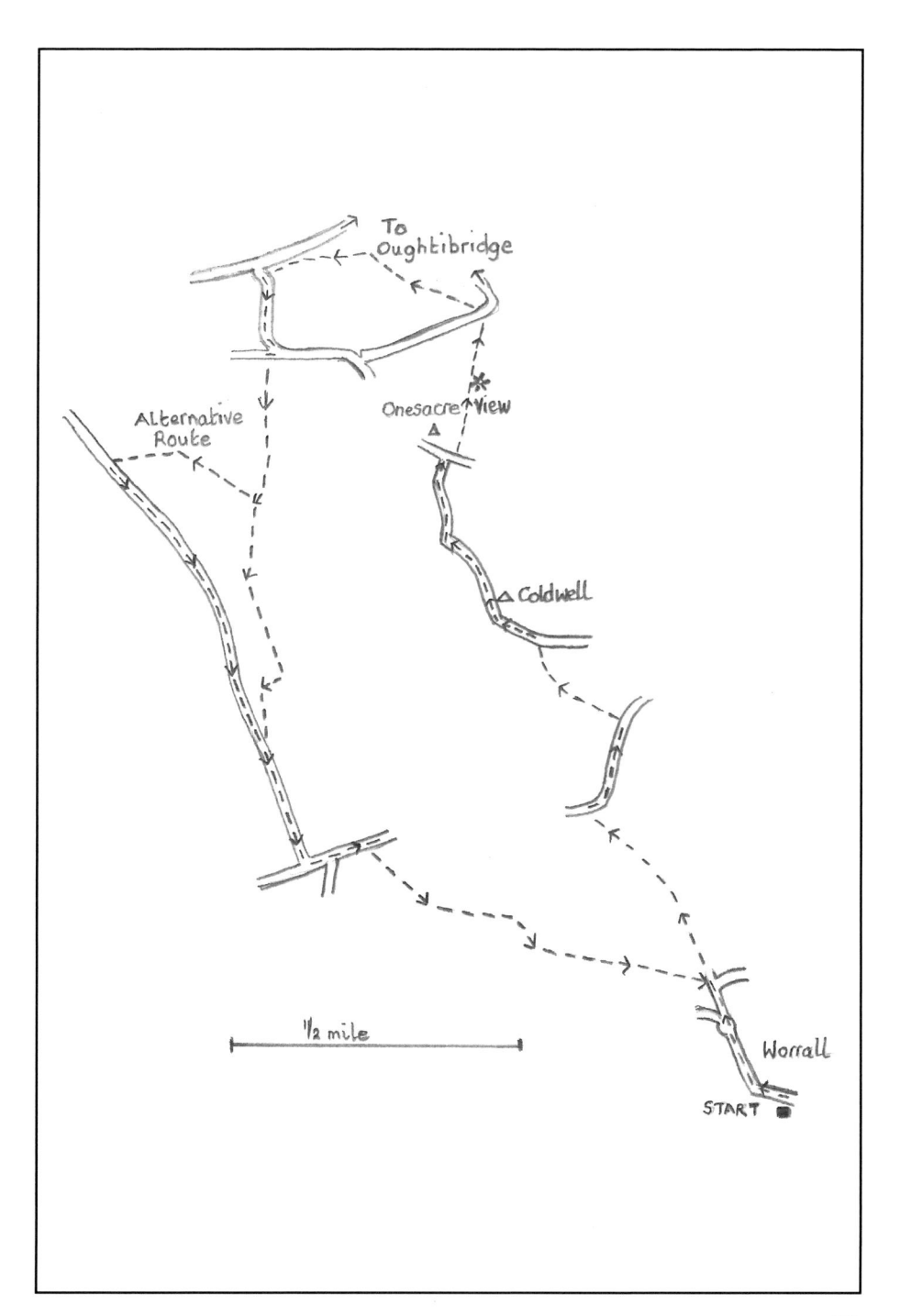

Walk Difficulty

In Winter, the field and woodland paths can be very muddy, but as well as this there are a number of other difficulties on this walk. There are several steep hills to climb, and there is also a tricky banking to get down soon after the start of the walk. There could also be also sheep and cows, and there a number of stiles to cross, some difficult.

Starting Point

Sycamore Park car park, Towngate Rd, Worrall, S35 0AR

The Route

Leave the car park to go left on to Towngate Road and follow the road to its end where there are 2 paths. Take the one straight across to go through fields, and as the path goes downhill head left towards trees. The path goes into the trees and down a difficult banking to reach Boggard Lane. Go left for a few yards to reach a road then double back right to walk along the road.

After a few minutes, the road reaches a farm on the left. Take a path which leads to the right of farm buildings, cutting through the farmyard to go downhill to the left, towards and then passing a small pond on the right. Walk across fields firstly keeping a wall on the right, then passing through a gap in the wall to keep in the same direction towards woods.

Into the bottom field the path goes straight across to reach a footbridge to cross a stream and then comes out on to Wheel Lane. Go left up the steep hill, and at the top at a 'T' junction take the path opposite which stays at the top of fields. This path heads towards stables in the distance on the right and leads to the left of the stables on to a road. Turn left up the road then after a few yards take a path right which goes through trees and into a field. The path heads towards trees on the other side of the field and then enters a small wood and turns left to go uphill. Further up, the path reaches Acre Lane near a road junction.

Turn left to go up Acre Lane to reach Limb Lane at the top at a junction. Go right for about 30 yards then take a path left into fields with a wall on the right. The path keeps in the same direction and eventually drops down to Coumes Wood. At the bottom, go through a gate on the right which heads into a dip as it enters the trees. Over a stream there are two choices. The path left can be extremely muddy for the first 200 yards, so a decision has to be made at this point whether to negotiate the mud, or whether to add 1.5 miles on to the walk by taking an alternative route through a beautiful, wooded section.

The first option then is to take the path left to go through the muddy wooded area to enter a field. In the field, go straight ahead keeping to the right of farm buildings to pick up a path in front of the woods which heads left towards the farm drive. Stay on the drive as it climbs and bends right and left to reach Onesmoor Bottom. Turn left to reach Burnt Hill Lane.

The alternative is to stay on the path which cuts uphill through the woods. The path picks up a wall to the right and stays close to it, with a stream on the other side of the wall as it bends right and steadily climbs to reach a stile in a wall. Over the stile the path bends left to reach the top of the woods. Here, ignore a path right to go straight across into fields and to immediately pass under power lines. At the top of the field the path comes out on to Onesmoor Bottom. Turn left to walk down the road to reach Burnt Hill Lane.

At the junction with Burnt Hill Lane go left for about 40 yards, then take a path right to cross several fields and a farm track, keeping in roughly the same direction to join up with a bridleway leading back to Towngate Road.

Look out for…..

Onesacre School House. Ecclesfield Parish records stated in 1835 that the school at Onesacre had an endowment of £14 per annum and a residence for the master, who taught sixteen children gratuitously.

Coldwell. The hamlet of Coldwell is so called because of the well outside the farm which is said to have extremely cold water running through it.

Onesacre. The little hamlet of Onesacre was mentioned in the Domesday Book in 1086. However, its history goes back to Anglo-Saxon times when it was part of the estate of the Saxon lord Godric. Onesacre was originally created as a forest clearing on high ground above the Don valley by Norwegian settlers, but after the Norman Conquest the Onesacre lands were owned by the Le Rous family who were of Norman descent.

Dog Suitability

Apart from the fields approaching Coumes Wood which may have sheep in them, the rest of the walk apart from the sections of road walking are perfect for dogs to be let off their leads. Apart from the amount of mud that there might be of course!

Refreshments

There are two pubs in Worrall for refreshments, the Shoulder of Mutton and the Blue Ball. There is also a village shop and post office there too.

Between Worrall and Oughtibridge is a small wood which this walk passes through, and at the edge of the wood, with a great view of the Upper Don Valley is this seat, with a plaque in the honour of a lady who loved the woods, and the view. The wood carvings and candles are an extra touch.

Walk No: 17 Shatton Moor

7 miles / 4 hours

Introduction

This walk is part Dark Peak part White Peak and whilst overlooking the Hope Valley it takes place on the opposite side of the valley to the more popular walking places which means that there are never as many people walking it. Much of the walk takes place on lanes and tracks which have good surfaces, making it quite an easy walk underfoot. However, there are sections which can be wet and muddy after rain, and there is a lot of climbing on this walk. The climb from Brough Lane to the top of the moor for instance is a mile and a half long and rises 230 metres (750 feet) along the way. The views on the way up are well worth the effort though; both looking up the valley towards Castleton and down to the village of Bradwell below from this lane which skirts Shatton Moor and Over Dale. From the high point of the walk the route descends to the village of Abney, then it's back up again across Offerton Moor to pass Offerton Hall before more country lanes to return to the start.

Walking group enjoying some shade on a hot day! Offerton Hall in the foreground with Hathersage behind and Stanage Edge in the distance

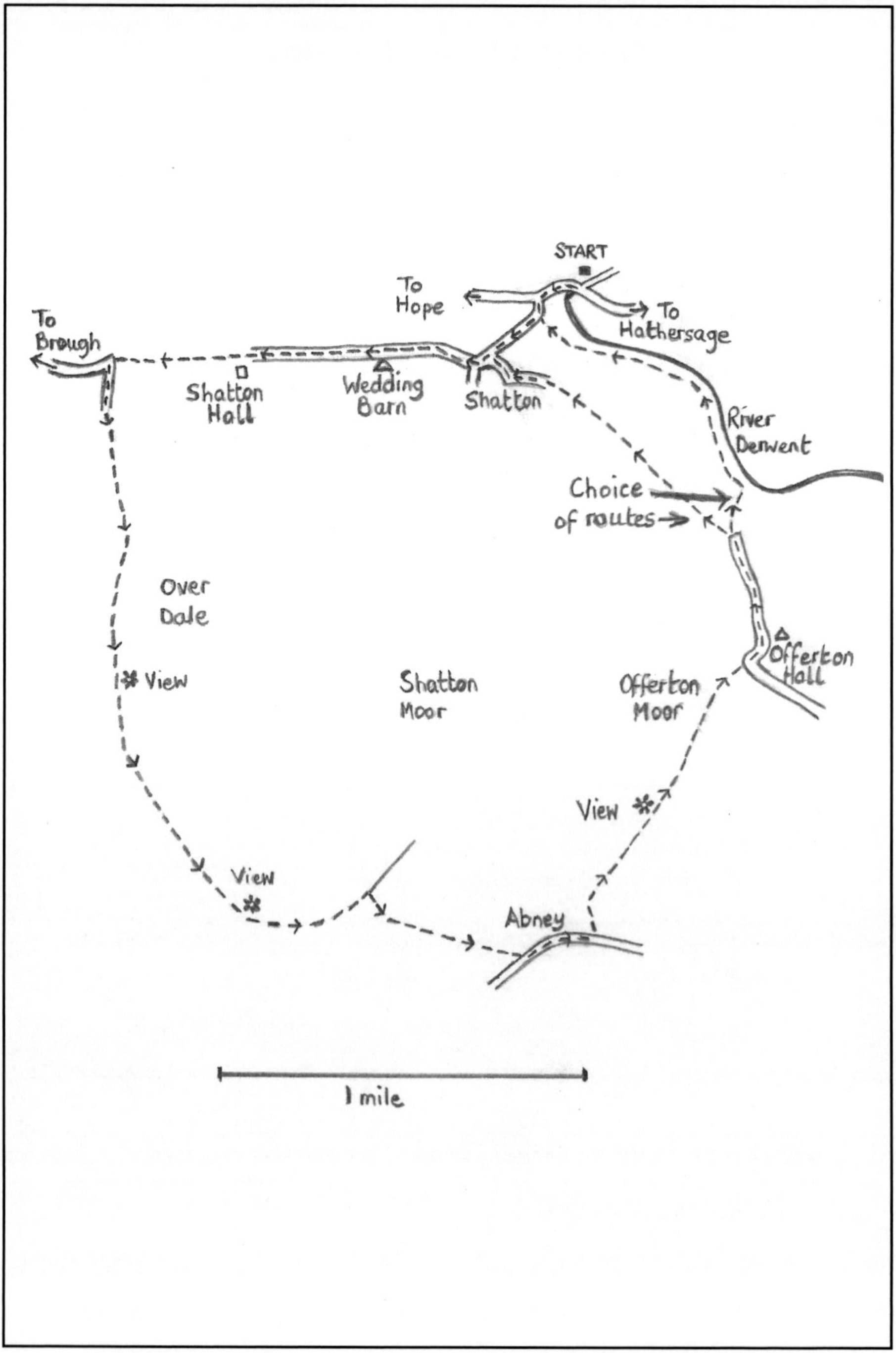
START
To Hope
To Hathersage
To Brough
Shatton Hall
Wedding Barn
Shatton
River Derwent
Choice of routes
Over Dale
View
Shatton Moor
Offerton Moor
Offerton Hall
View
View
Abney
1 mile

Walk Difficulty

This walk is best suited to people who have attempted 7-mile walks with high climbs before. Although the paths are mainly good, and there isn't a single stile, the climb from the valley would tax the best of walkers. There are some steep grass bankings which can be slippery on the return leg too.

Starting Point

Mytham Bridge is the starting point chosen for this walk as there is plenty of roadside parking there. There are also a couple of spaces at the bottom of Shatton Lane, just over the bridge from Hope Road as an alternative. Mytham Bridge is the name of a road in Bamford and the postcode for it is S33 0EA.

The Route

Turn right along the main road and cross just before the first bend to go over Shatton Bridge, continuing along Shatton Lane as it bends right. Heading uphill, 200 yards after the last houses go up steps on the left to take a path on the edge of a field which runs parallel to the lane. After passing the wedding barn the path rejoins the lane further up. At the drive for Shatton Hall go right through a gate to carry on in the same direction on a path which enters woods, then further on reaches Brough Lane at a bend in the lane.

Turn left to walk up the lane as it becomes a rough track and keeps rising above Over Dale on the left, and Bradwell and the Hope Valley on the right. After levelling off the track bends left, then after a few hundred yards reaches the top of a narrow, tarmacked lane on the right. Go right down the lane until it emerges into the centre of Abney. Turn left to walk through the village, then 100 yards after the last house go through a gate on the left, followed by another gate on to an enclosed path leading uphill.

The path soon bends right and goes through 2 gates to lead on to scrubland, and then upwards on to Offerton Moor. Crossing the moor and keeping in the same direction, go straight across at cross paths to reach the top of the moor before dropping down the other side towards a road. The path bends right towards and approaching the road there is a feint path left which leads over a stile and on to the road. It is easy to miss this path and arrive at a gate to the road instead. The gate is fairly easy to climb over if this happens!

Turn left and stay on the road as it bends a few times and goes downhill passing Offerton Hall, until after about half a mile it ends at a farm drive. There are 2 choices here. If the paths so far have been exceptionally muddy, take the track to the left and stay on it keeping in the same direction as it becomes a road further on at a farm on the left. Continue on the road as it leads back into Shatton, then turn right to take Shatton Lane back to the start. The alternative is to take a path next to the farm drive which goes to the left of the farm and leads down to the River Derwent. Turn left here on to a path which is often very muddy and stay on it to return to Shatton.

Look out for…..

Shatton means 'farmstead in the nook of land between streams', which describes this hamlet perfectly as it sits beside the confluence of the Derwent and Noe. Townfield Lane which leads away from Shatton is an ancient route which was part of a salter's lane which ran from Sheffield to Cheshire.

Wedding Barn on Townfield Lane at Shatton. Great place for a wedding do!

Offerton Hall. There has been a house on this site since the 12th century. In 1415, Nicholas Eyre re-built the house following his return from the Battle of Agincourt where he fought alongside his father. Offerton is one of a group of seven houses Robert Eyre built in and around Hathersage, one for each of his seven sons and all within sight of the others and his own new home, North Lees Hall – used by Charlotte Bronte later on as the model for Thornfield in her novel Jane Eyre. The other houses were at Moorseats, Highlow, Shatton, Nether Shatton, Hazelford, and Crookhill.

Dog Suitability

For the 2.5 miles from the woods just after Shatton Hall to the village of Abney, dogs can be off lead for almost all the way but that's it for the rest of the walk as it is either country lanes or the possibility of animals in fields for the other 4.5 miles. A good thing is that there are no stiles at all on this walk.

Refreshments

Apart from pubs and shops in Bamford a short drive away, the petrol station at Sickleholme has a shop for refreshments, and there is also the excellent café at the High Peak Garden Centre at the start of the walk.

Walk No: 18 Burbage Moor

4.5 miles / 2 hours

Introduction

This walk takes place entirely inside the Peak District, but also within the Sheffield city boundary. There are no serious hills on the walk and no stiles so it isn't too difficult a walk but some of the paths are quite stony, and in winter especially, the section through Burbage Moor can be boggy, so stout boots are a must. The route starts by walking along Houndkirk Road for a while before crossing Burbage Moor to reach Burbage Edge. From there, the return to the start is via the Ox Stones rock formation and Lady Canning's Plantation. There are great views throughout the walk, looking towards the south of Sheffield on the first leg, then at Burbage Edge there are more fine vistas looking across the valley at Higgar Tor, Carl Wark and the Hope Valley.

View of Sheffield city centre from Houndkirk Road at Ringinglow

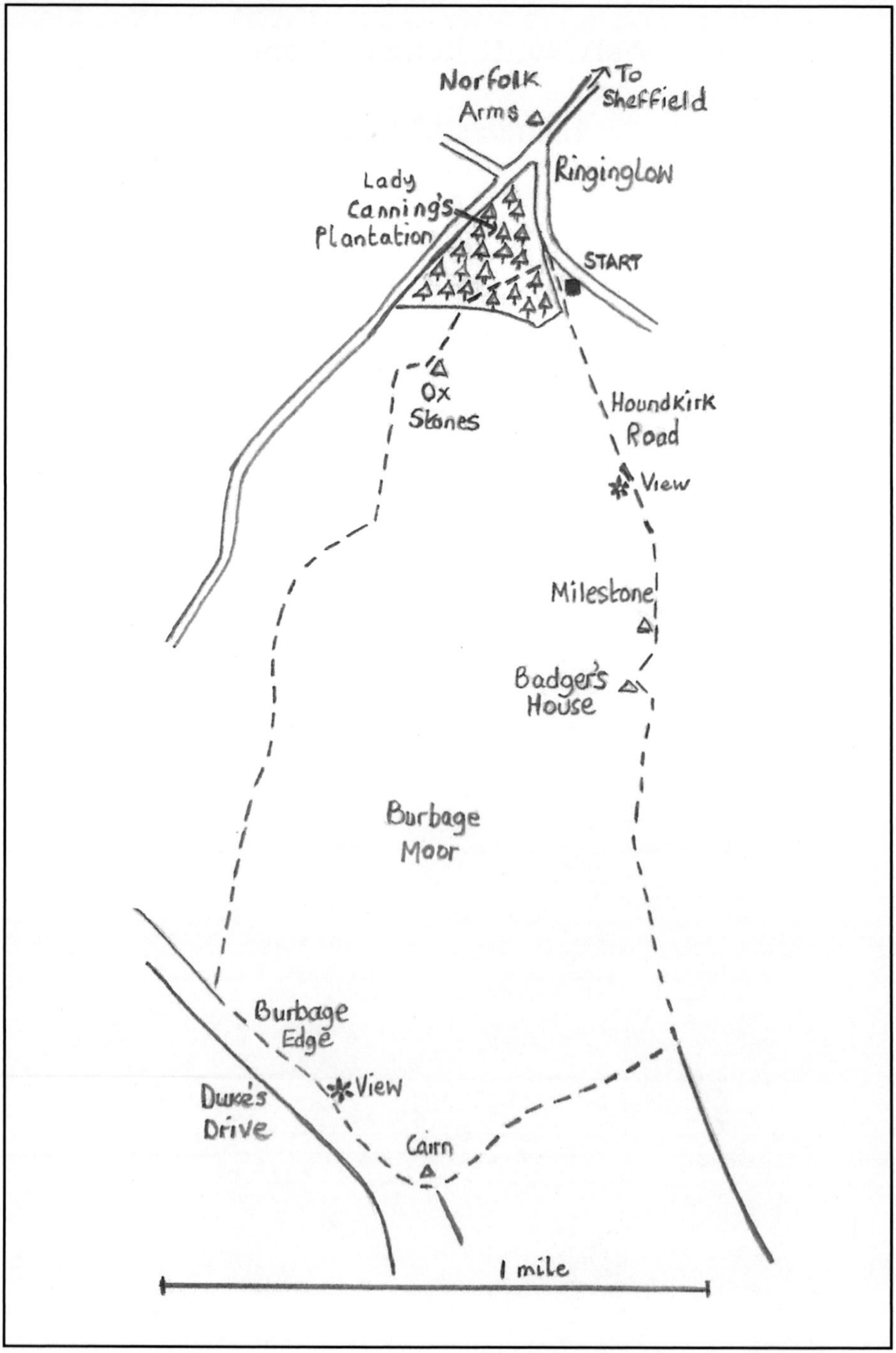
Norfolk Arms
To Sheffield
Ringinglow
Lady Canning's Plantation
START
Ox Stones
Houndkirk Road
View
Milestone
Badger's House
Burbage Moor
Burbage Edge
View
Duke's Drive
Cairn
1 mile

Walk Difficulty

There are a couple of short inclines, both in the first half of the walk, but neither of them are too difficult. The paths are very rocky though, so care must be taken on the Houndkirk Road and Burbage Edge sections. There's also the possibility of mud and standing water after rain, particularly across Burbage Moor.

Starting Point

Lady Canning's MTB Trail Parking, Sheffield S11 7TU is the starting point for this walk. A simple instruction to find this parking area is to go to the Norfolk Arms on Ringinglow Road, turn left on to Sheephill Road, then after 300 yards, as the road bends left, go straight forward on to Houndkirk Road and the car parking area is immediately on the left.

The Route

From the parking area turn left to walk up Houndkirk Road. Stay on this old road for a mile and a half to reach a gate on the right by a signpost, just before a short rise. Go through the gate on to a path which climbs up until after just over 300 yards it reaches another gate. Through the gate the path carries on in the same direction going downhill slightly until after ¼ of a mile it reaches a fork.

Go right here, then after 50 yards reach a junction of paths at a cairn. Go right again to walk on the top of Burbage Edge towards Upper Burbage Bridge. Stay on this path for ¾ of a mile then look for an unsignposted path on the right just after a second gas warning sign.

Take this feint path through the moor as it runs parallel to Ringinglow Road a few hundred yards away for quite a while. In the distance on the right the Ox Stones rock formation can be seen which is where the route heads. At the path looks like it's going to come out on to Ringinglow Road it bears right, then after a total distance of a mile it reaches two rock formations.

Pass the first set of rocks to reach the second set which is the Ox Stones. Take a path to the left here which heads down towards Lady Canning's Plantation. Ignoring a path left the path reaches a gate leading on to a track going left and right. Go through the gate, then another gate opposite to enter the plantation. Walk all the way through the plantation to emerge back on to Houndkirk Road to reach the car parking area.

Look out for.....

Ringinglow which is supposed to have got its name after a man lost on the moors in bad weather was saved when he heard the bells of Sheffield Parish Church 'ringing low' over the moors.

Houndkirk Road was part of the Sheffield to Hathersage turnpike, which was an early road through the Peak District, and was improved by a turnpike trust in the 18th century. The road is thought to have originated as a Roman road. It stopped being used as a road in the 1930's when the Sheffield to Fox House road was opened.

Milestone from @ 1767 on Houndkirk Road which is situated on the right just before the bridge. Until recently it sat in the garden of a Dore resident for 70 years and was discovered after their death. Along with most signposts in the country it was removed in WW2 so would be invaders would get confused!

Badgers House was situated just beyond the milestone. It was built in 1822 and began life as a pub to serve travellers. Later in 19c it was converted into two cottages, and demolished in the 1930's.

Duke's Drive, also known as Green Drive, which runs up the valley between Burbage Edge and Higgar Tor. It was built by the Duke of Rutland in the 1820's to lead shooting parties to the grouse moors. The Duke owned Longshaw Lodge which was built for entertaining and accommodation. There have been a number of archeological finds in the valley close to the drive, including Bronze Age cairns and burial chambers.

Lady Canning's Plantation is thought to have been named after Joan, the 1st Lady Canning whose husband was briefly Prime Minister in the early 1800's. She was sister-in-law to the Duke of Portland, who was the grandson of the 4th Duke of Devonshire who owned land nearby, so possibly that's where it came from, but no-one knows for sure!

Dog Suitability

A few hundred yards after the start of the walk a gate is reached, and from this point the walk enters an area where dogs must be kept under a close control until near the end of the walk when it enters Lady Canning's Plantation. There are sheep in this area and the rule regarding dog control is particularly necessary in lambing season from 1st March to 31st July.

Refreshments

The Norfolk Arms pub at Ringinglow, and a café at the Alpaca Farm on Fulwood Lane are not far from the start of the walk.

Walking group in the heather on Burbage Moor

Walk No: 19 Our Cow Molly

7.75 miles / 4 hours

Introduction

This is another tough 7 ¾ mile walk which would be best suited to experienced walkers. Starting with a climb high above the Rivelin Valley there are ups and downs all through the walk which takes place on mainly little-used paths and tracks, some of which were ancient pack horse routes. Two of Sheffield's rivers feature in this walk too, the Rivelin and the Loxley, with much evidence of their industrial pasts along with further history at Underbank chapel and school room on the way back. And of course, as the route passes through the Our Cow Molly dairy there is the chance to sample their sumptuous ices. On a clear day, there are fantastic views throughout the walk to enjoy.

Field paths leading from Stannington down to the Rivelin Valley

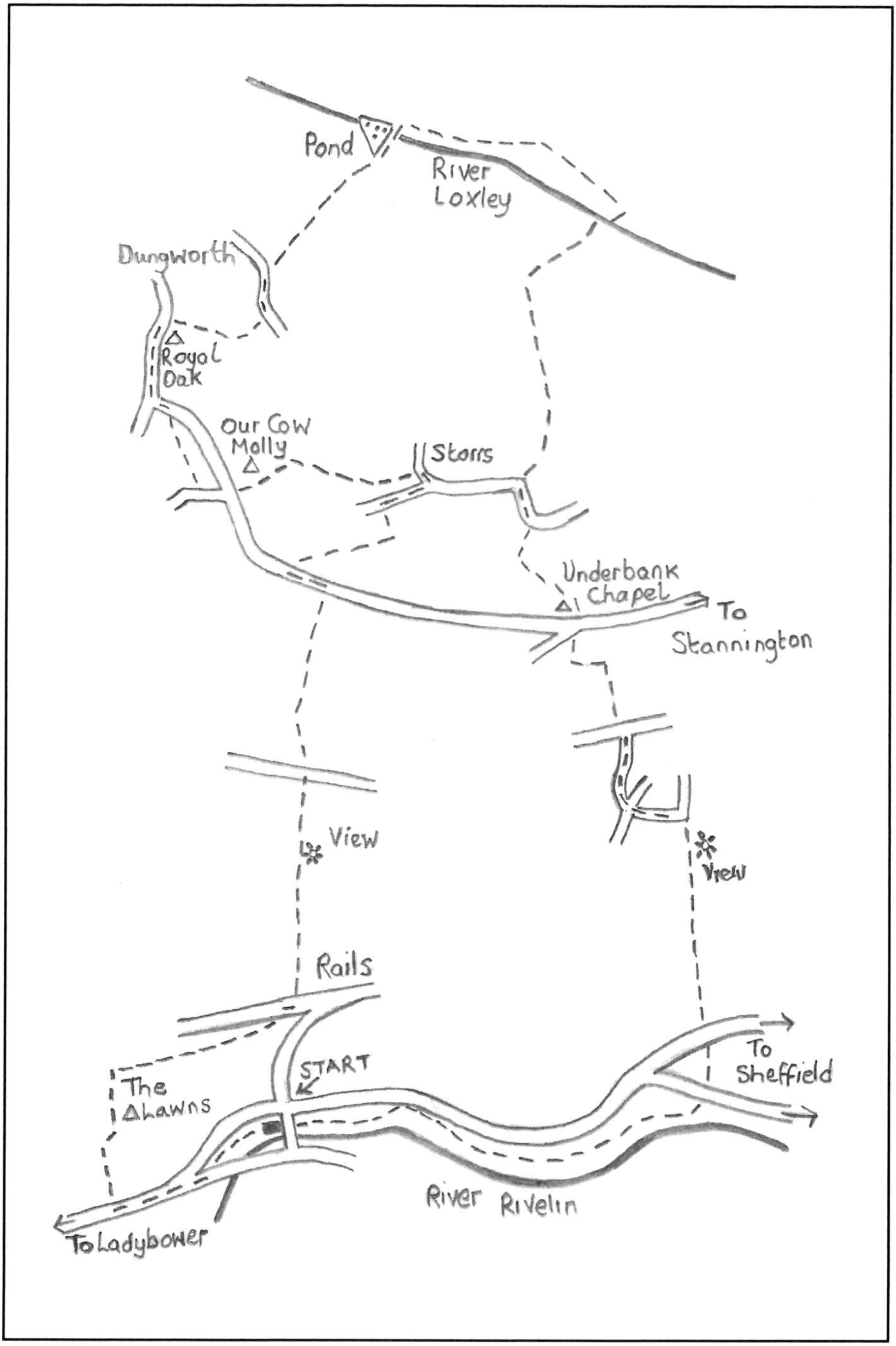
Pond
River Loxley
Dungworth
Royal Oak
Our Cow Molly
Storrs
Underbank Chapel
To Stannington
View
View
Rails
START
The Lawns
To Sheffield
River Rivelin
To Ladybower

Walk Difficulty

Lots of climbs and numerous stiles, some of which are difficult, are some of the reasons which make this quite a difficult walk. There are also one or two tricky downhill sections where there could be loose stones and which could be slippery after rain, and there is also the possibility of mud and standing water. Watch out too for tree roots and overhanging branches in the woodland sections, and some of the fields may have sheep, cows, and horses.

Starting Point

Rails Road car park, Rails Rd, Sheffield S6 6GF

The Route

From the car park take the path leading away from the road to come out on to Manchester Road. Turn right, cross Rivelin Valley Road at the junction then after 100 yards turn right at a footpath sign to go up a driveway towards a farm. Approaching the farm take a path which leads uphill to the left of the farm. Into the woods, go right on a path which after about 5 minutes comes out on to a road. A few yards right, take a path left which leads up a field with a wall on the right. Further up at a path crossroads carry on upwards to reach another road. Cross the road to take a path downhill with trees on the right.

Further down, cross a track to keep in the same direction passing new houses on the right. At the next road go left for 100 yards, then take a lane on the right which soon becomes a path and eventually bends left to reach a road. Go right along this road to a 'T' junction in the hamlet of Storrs, then walk left for 40 yards to then take a track left alongside houses. Pass a farm on the left on to fields which head in the direction of 2 white gates in the distance. Go through the smaller gate and turn left to reach and pass Our Cow Molly farm.

Cross the main road, then after 100 yards go right on to a drive which leads on to footpaths which go round converted dwellings. Stay on this path as it heads downhill to reach a road. Go left along this road into Dungworth, then take a path on the right at the side of the Royal Oak. This path is little-used and a bit overgrown and heads downhill in the direction of a cottage which has a smallholding. After going through a squeeze stile left, the path leads to a road. Go left along the road for 50 yards then take a path right through a gate. The path leads through trees with a stream on the right to reach a wall. Through the wall head to the right corner of the field and into woods.

Go over a bridge and up steps to reach a fence where the path leads left to cross another bridge to reach a fishing pond. Go right past the pond on a path which leads to an old road through disused buildings. Just before the road bends left take a path on the right to follow the river. Passing more disused buildings on the right, then a dam on left, the path leads towards more disused buildings and a road. Turn right in this industrial area to cross a bridge over the river heading towards a row of houses. Pass to the left of the houses picking up a path which heads above the houses into woods.

After 75 yards take a narrow path right at a signpost which heads uphill through woods. At the top of the woods go over a stile to turn left to go over another stile next to a gate. Turn left to walk along the edge of a field, then cross the next 2 fields diagonally. At the top corner of the second field, cross a stile on to a path which bends right alongside a fence to reach another 2 stiles in quick succession. A short green lane leads to a path between houses and on to Storrs Lane. Turn left to walk down the road, then at a sharp left bend go straight forward on to a track which crosses a brook.

Keep on the track as it climbs up to Stannington Road. Go right here for 50 yards, passing Underbank Chapel to take a minor road left. After a few yards take a path left, then as it climbs bear left to reach a ridge going left. At a gate, go right on to a path up a field with a wall on the left. At a road, cross over to walk down Reynard Road for 100 yards to reach a crossroads. Cross on to Nethergate, then where the road bends left take a path on the right leading downhill through fields to a minor road. Cross the road, then soon after cross Rivelin Valley Road to a path opposite. Go right to drop down to the valley from where the car park is just under a mile. Turn right and after a short while there are options to walk along the valley to return to the start. The one chosen for this book is the easiest one!

In just under half a mile, after passing two dams take a right fork to climb up to the road. At the road, there is a path a few yards ahead which leads back down to the valley, and then on to Rails Road opposite the car park.

Look out for…..

The Lawns which is famous for the find of a rare Roman diploma in 1761. It is a brass military diploma dated from A.D. 124 awarded by the Emperor Hadrian to an unknown man whose home was in Belgium. The type of diploma it is indicates that this person had been a foot soldier and had served at least twenty-five campaigns in the Roman army.

Our Cow Molly farm was established in 1947 by Hector Andrew who started out with 10 cows to produce milk to deliver to local shops and homes. In 2007, Our Cow Molly started using its own milk and cream to produce ice cream and then a bit later came the ice cream parlour.

Underbank Chapel was built in 1743 to replace the first chapel built on this site in 1652. The schoolroom opposite was built as a school in 1854 at a cost of £600. After it took 31 years for the debt taken on in the building of the school to be paid off, the school was closed 25 years later in 1910.

Rivelin Valley Industry. The river was used to turn many waterwheels that powered the steel and cutlery industries, forge, paper mills and corn mills. A three-mile stretch of the lower Rivelin valley had 20 watermills and 21 mill dams, working from the 16th to 20th centuries.

Dog Suitability

In the sections through the valleys dogs can be off-lead, and through the wooded areas too, but the usual rules apply regarding keeping your dog under control in the fields where there are animals.

Refreshments

Refreshments on this walk are available at the Royal Oak at Dungworth and Our Cow Molly farm.

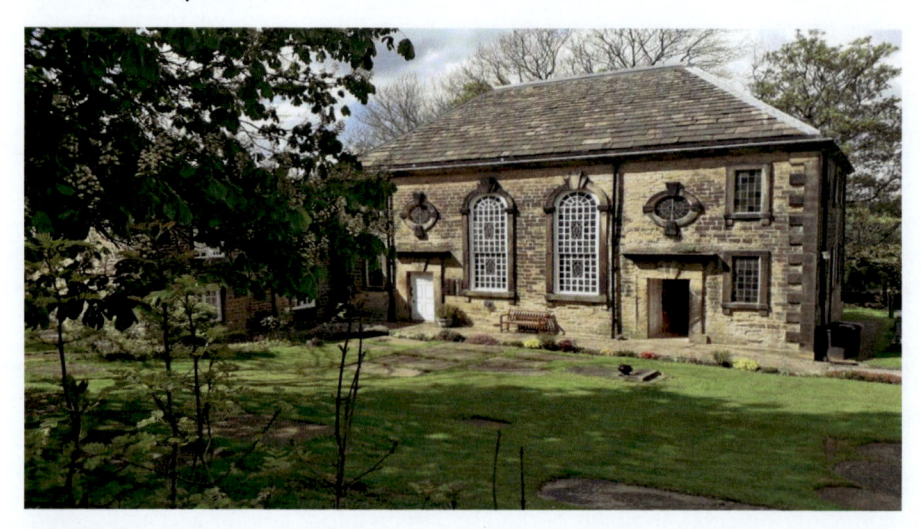

Underbank Chapel

Walk No: 20 Blacka Moor

4 miles / 2 hours

Introduction

This is another walk which is both just inside the Sheffield boundary and also just inside the Peak District National Park. Blacka Moor Nature Reserve is a lovely place to walk, with its flora and fauna, especially as it might be possible to spot red deer during the walk. There is also a surprisingly lot of history at various places on the route, making the walk an interesting one from that point of view too. It's not an easy walk though mainly thanks to the rocky paths, and the long climb to get on to Totley Moor after leaving Blacka Moor. The rewards from the views as the route climbs though are well worth the effort of getting up there. After leaving the nature reserve the uphill section uses an old packhorse road, and part of the Sheffield Country Walk from the outskirts of Totley to pass Brown Edge on the way back to the start.

Autumn in Blacka Moor Nature Reserve

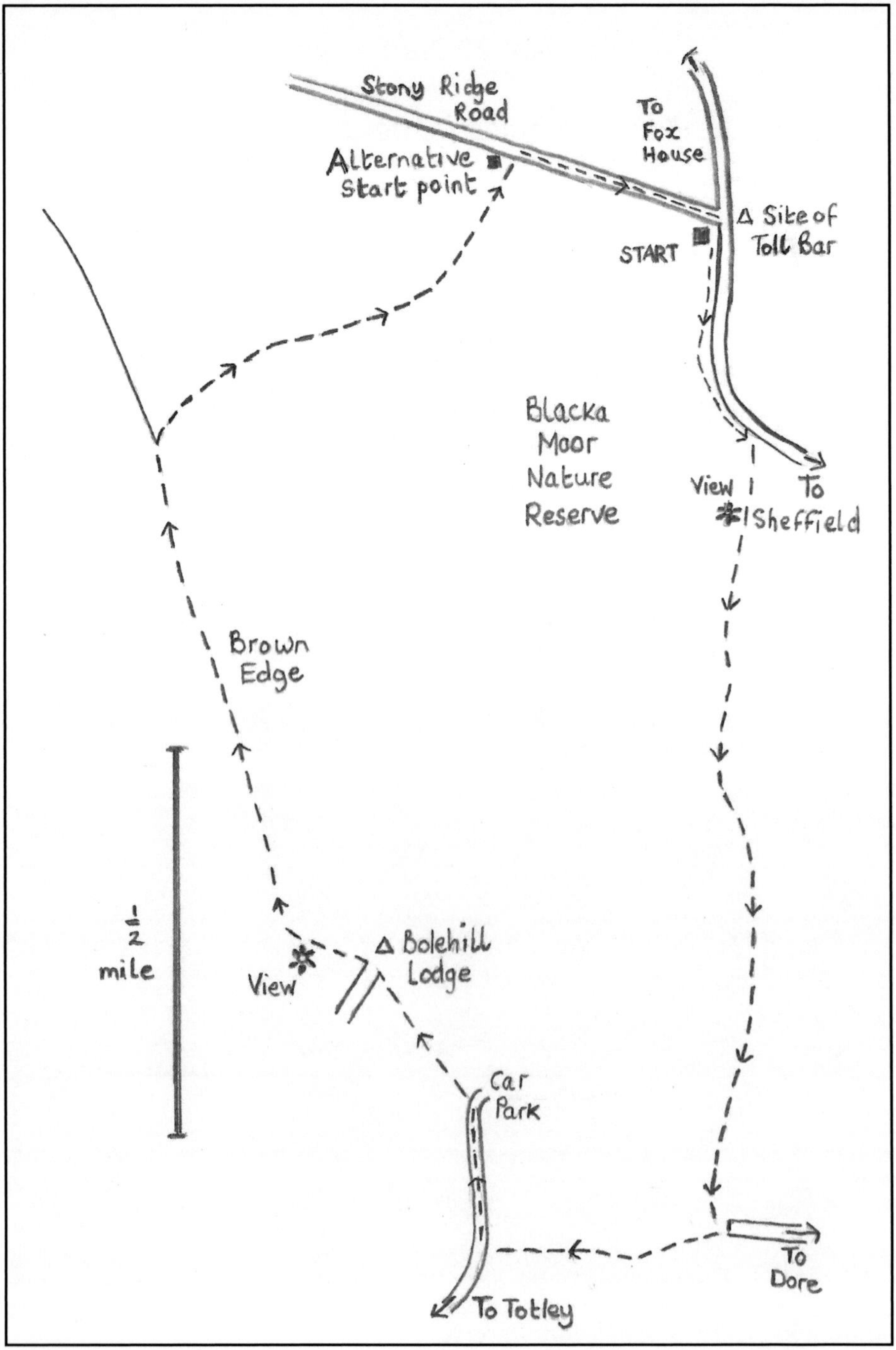

Stony Ridge Road
To Fox House
Alternative Start point
Site of Toll Bar
START
Blacka Moor Nature Reserve
View
To Sheffield
Brown Edge
1/2 mile
Bolehill Lodge
View
Car Park
To Dore
To Totley

Walk Difficulty

Whilst walking through the nature reserve care must be taken on the uneven paths leading downhill which are steep in parts, and also have protruding tree roots. The path leading on to Totley Moor known as Moss Road is fairly steep uphill for half a mile, and when it flattens out the path for the remainder of the walk can be muddy and having standing water after rain.

Starting Point

There are two choices, both very close to each other. There is a small car park, Stony Ridge Car Park, Hathersage Road, Sheffield S17 3BJ. Or the walk can be started 0.3 miles along Stony Ridge Road from Hathersage Road where there is parking roadside next to a path which is on the walk route.

The Route

Starting from Stony Ridge Car park take the first path on the left into woods. The path runs parallel to the road for about half a mile, passing through a gate until it reaches a signpost. Turn right here to head downhill. This next section is where there are mostly to be red deer. Ignore any paths left and right to carry on downhill for half a mile until a path joins this one from the left as the path flattens out.

Keeping in the same direction the path becomes a track, and then further on a tarmacked road as it rounds a left-hand bend. Take the footpath signed to the right to enter a field which leads down a hill. At the bottom of the field cross a footbridge to go through a squeeze stile to a narrow path between walls. At the lane at the top of steps turn right on to a short stretch of road which passes Hallfield Farm and then ends at a car park on the right.

Take a track on the left here known as Moss Road to climb steeply. The track passes a road opposite Bolehill Lodge on the right, and then just under a mile after this, at wooden fencing on the right, there is a fork right which has a sign for Sheffield Country Walk. Take this and keep on it to reach Stony Ridge Road. Turn right and walk along the road to return to the car park.

Look out for…..

Stony Ridge Toll Bar had a toll house which was situated across the road from the car park and took a toll for the carriage of beer, coal, flour and millstones on this turnpike road between Sheffield and Hathersage. Built in 1816, it was demolished in 1919 after tolls ended in 1884.

Blacka Moor. Unique features on Blacka Moor include the varied heather, it's diversity of grassland, heathland, wetland and woodland, and its population of milberry bumblebees. Its migrant bird population includes willow warblers, black caps, cuckoos, wheatears, stonechats, and whinchats. There are also red deer on the moor.

Bolehill Lodge is currently a holiday property but was built in 1841 as a shooting lodge. Totley Bole Hill is situated just behind the lodge and is one of the best medieval lead smelting sites in England. Bole hills were places where lead was smelted in the open air, and they were normally usually situated at or near the top of a hill where the wind was strong, which is why Totley Bole Hill is situated where it is. It is thought to have operated from the medieval period until the 16th century.

Sheffield Country Walk is made up of 22 sections and is 53 miles long, covering the outskirts of Sheffield.

Brown Edge. A fire a few years ago revealed a large number of flint knives, blades, arrowheads and scrapers left behind by people from the Stone Age. The large number of arrowheads suggests that the moors were their hunting grounds.

Dog Suitability

On most of the route dogs can be off lead. There is just one field at Totley where there could be animals, and there is a small amount of road walking too. On Totley Moor there could be a few sheep in the distance, so dogs need to be kept under control on this part. There are only 2 stiles on the walk.

Refreshments

There is nowhere en route or nearby for refreshments, the nearest places are the Fox House pub, and pubs and shops at Totley and Dore.

Walk No: 21 Eyam

8 miles / 4 hours

Introduction

This is a fairly easy 8 mile walk which from the starting point at Calver quickly leads through the little-known Coombs Dale and then on to various fields and tracks to reach the plague village of Eyam. The return section of the walk goes through more fields as it passes the Boundary Stone on the way to the pretty village of Stoney Middleton, and then back to Calver on more tracks and field paths. As well as the plague-related history in Eyam, other highlights of the walk are a fluorspar mine, a highwayman's tale, a couple of old packhorse tracks and one of only six octagonal shaped churches in the country. There are also great views of the limestone-walled fields which make up this lovely part of the White Peak.

Looking towards Foolow with Bretton in the distance on the way to Eyam

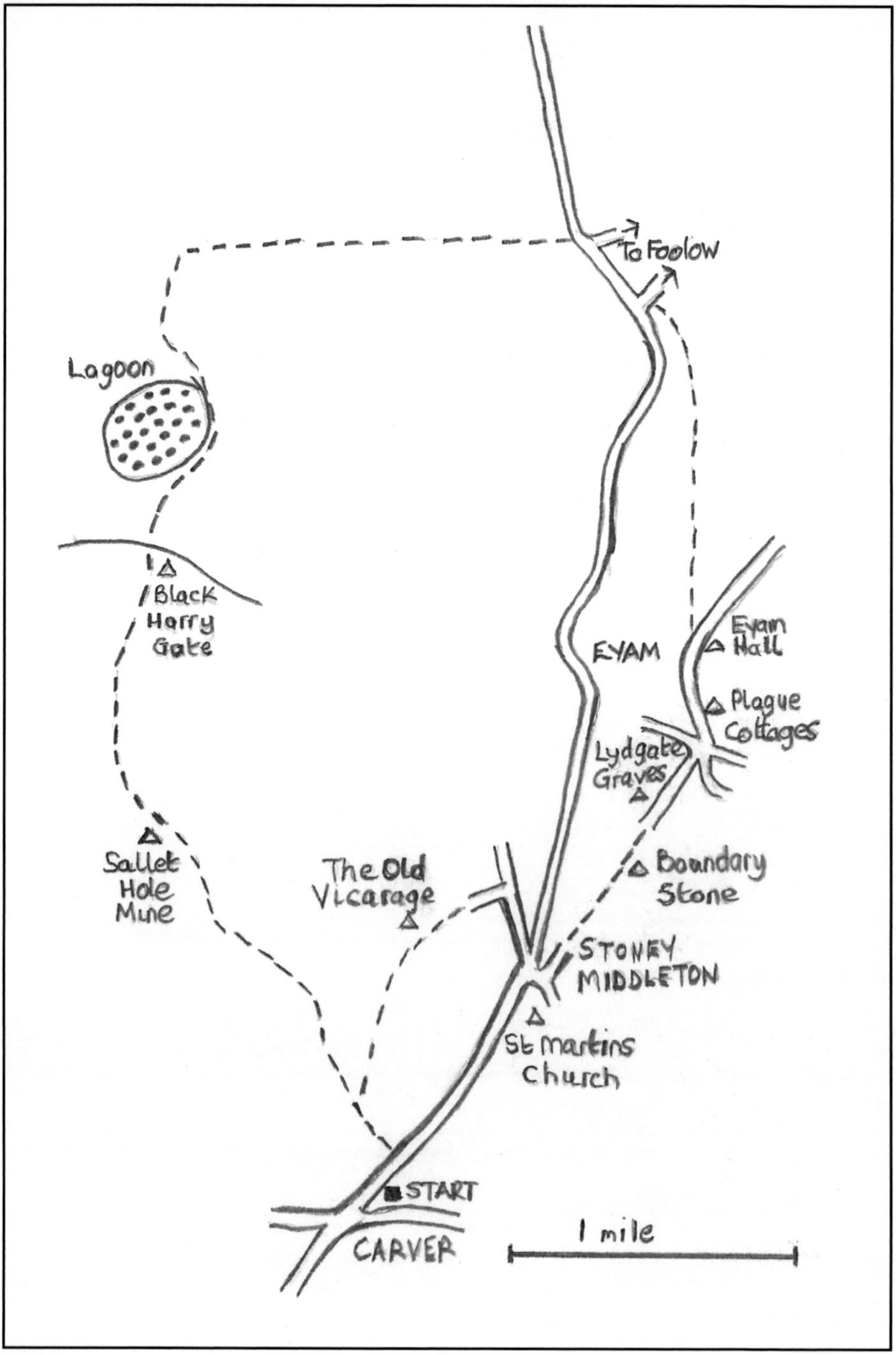
To Foolow
Lagoon
Black
Harry
Gate
EYAM
Eyam
Hall
Plague
Cottages
Lydgate
Graves
Sallet
Hole
Mine
The Old
Vicarage
Boundary
Stone
STONEY
MIDDLETON
St martins
Church
START
CARVER
1 mile

Walk Difficulty

There's not a lot to watch out for on this walk, just the potential for the Coombes Dale path to be wet and slippery after rain, and the number of stiles there are throughout the walk. There is also a grass banking on the way down to Stoney Middleton where a bit of care needs to be taken.

Starting Point

There is limited parking for the start of this walk on Polly Froggatt Lane, and also on Sough Lane, both being just off the crossroads at Calver. The address of the Eyre Arms on the crossroads is Chesterfield Road, Calver, S32 3XH.

The Route

From the crossroads in Calver, walk 450 yards along the Stoney Middleton road, and then take a track on the left at the side of a sports field. Stay on the track through Coombs Dale for just over 2 miles to reach a track going left and right. This cross-track point is called Black Harry Gate, with Black Harry Lane going right here. Keep straight on as the path bends left further on to go round a lagoon on the left. After ¾ of a mile the path reaches a track right.

After a few minutes on the track it reaches a road. A few yards to the right take a path right which crosses a number of fields. With a farm up ahead on the right, cross a lane, and then the farm access drive to keep to the left of a small wood, and to the left of the farm. Follow a wall as it curves right, then take a stile beside gates. Keep in the same direction through more fields to reach the main road at the side of a row of houses. Turn right along the main road, and then after 100 yards cross the road at a road junction on the left to take a track on the right which leads to Eyam.

After just over a mile the track arrives at houses and becomes a tarmacked road. Soon after this look for a signposted path on the right and take this path which after crossing a road and passing through a small housing estate leads into the centre of Eyam. At the main road turn right to walk along the road and just after the school take the left fork to arrive at The Square.

At a 'T' junction cross over to take a narrow lane opposite called Lydgate. The lane winds upwards through cottages then just after passing Mill Lane on the left the lane ends and becomes a path which leads into a field. Stay on the path going over stiles and through gates as the path passes the Boundary Stone as it leads through fields down towards Stoney Middleton.

After ¾ of a mile the path reaches a lane. Turn right and stay on the lane as it bends left and then joins another lane to carry on downhill to finally bend right to reach the main road. Cross the road on to a road opposite which goes to the right of the Moon Inn. After around 200 yards of climbing up this short, steep hill take a minor road left, Eaton Fold. The road soon becomes a track and carries on rising to give great views of the valley below. After ¼ of a mile, just after the third gate, fork left on to a path which after around 100 yards reaches the track used just after the start of the walk. Turn left to reach the main road and then turn right to return to the start.

Look out for…..

Sallet Hole Mine. Found half way up Coombs Dale this fluorspar mine closed in 1996. Fluorspar is the mineral name of calcium fluoride, and industrially it is used in smelting, and in the production of glasses and enamels.

Black Harry Gate. Black Harry was a highwayman of the 18th century who preyed on travellers. Many of the routes of this area converge on the junction of Black Harry Gate. Black Harry Lane to the right is one of a series of packhorse ways used from the early Middle-Ages until the mid-nineteenth century to transport goods across the Peak District. Merchants whose goods were delivered by packhorse generally collected payment in person. These men were prized prey, riding home with their golden guineas along bridle-ways and through fields where frequent gibbets, or gallows warned them of their perils.

Blakedon Hollow Lagoon at the top of Coombs Dale was built to treat the waste from the fluorspar industry on the site of Black Harry Farm which was demolished in the 1970s.

Eyam Hall built 6 years after the Eyam plague in 1672 by Thomas Wright was given to his son John as a wedding present. This Jacobean house has been owned by 11 generations of the Wright family right up to the present day. The hall and its walled gardens are open to the public, and the old stable yard houses a number of local craft and food shops.

Plague Cottages are where the plague broke out and where the first deaths of the plague occurred. Each cottage has a plaque about the family that lived there and the affect the plague had on them. It was in the Plague Cottage itself where George Viccars opened the fateful package containing the deadly fleas that would doom the village of Eyam for the next 12 months.

Lydgate Graves are halfway up Lydgate, a narrow lane the route passes through in Eyam. As the churchyard was banned during the plague, people who needed to bury their dead had to bury the victims by themselves. Around the village there are various graves, and the Lydgate graves are where members of the Darby family were interred after falling victim to the plague. Two small gravestones are dedicated to Mary and her father George.

The Boundary Stone. During the outbreak of the plague when the inhabitants of Eyam quarantined themselves, villagers would come to place money in six holes drilled into the top of the boundary stone to pay for food and medicine left by neighbours from other villages close by.

Saint Martins Church in Stoney Middleton which is unique for its octagonal shaped nave. It was built in 1415 by Joan Eyre in thanksgiving for the safe return from the Battle of Agincourt of her husband Robert. The original Tower still stands but the nave was destroyed by fire in 1757.

The Old Vicarage in Stoney Middleton which was built towards the end of the Georgian period and is Grade ll listed.

Dog Suitability

Most of the walk is suitable for dogs to be off lead, apart from the section from Eyam to Stoney Middleton where there could be sheep.

Refreshments

There is a selection of shops and pubs at Carver, Eyam and Stoney Middleton.

Lydgate graves in Eyam

Walk No: 22 Oaking Clough

5.25 miles / 2.5 hours

Introduction

There are a lot of cloughs in the Peak District; a clough being a steep sided ravine or narrow valley. Oaking Clough isn't that special on its own, but what does make it special is that there is a small reservoir important to Sheffield's growth in the early 1800's, and strange derelict waterboard houses up there. Oaking Clough is in the Redmires area of Sheffield, and the Upper Redmires reservoir is the starting point for the walk. From there, the walk heads off over Hallam Moors, which is where most of the walk takes place, and includes the highest section of the Redmires Conduit. From the conduit it's on to Stanage Edge via a whole series of grouse butts and shelters to return to the start via Long Causeway and Stanedge Pole to reach the upper reservoir again.

Derelict waterboard houses at Oaking Clough reservoir

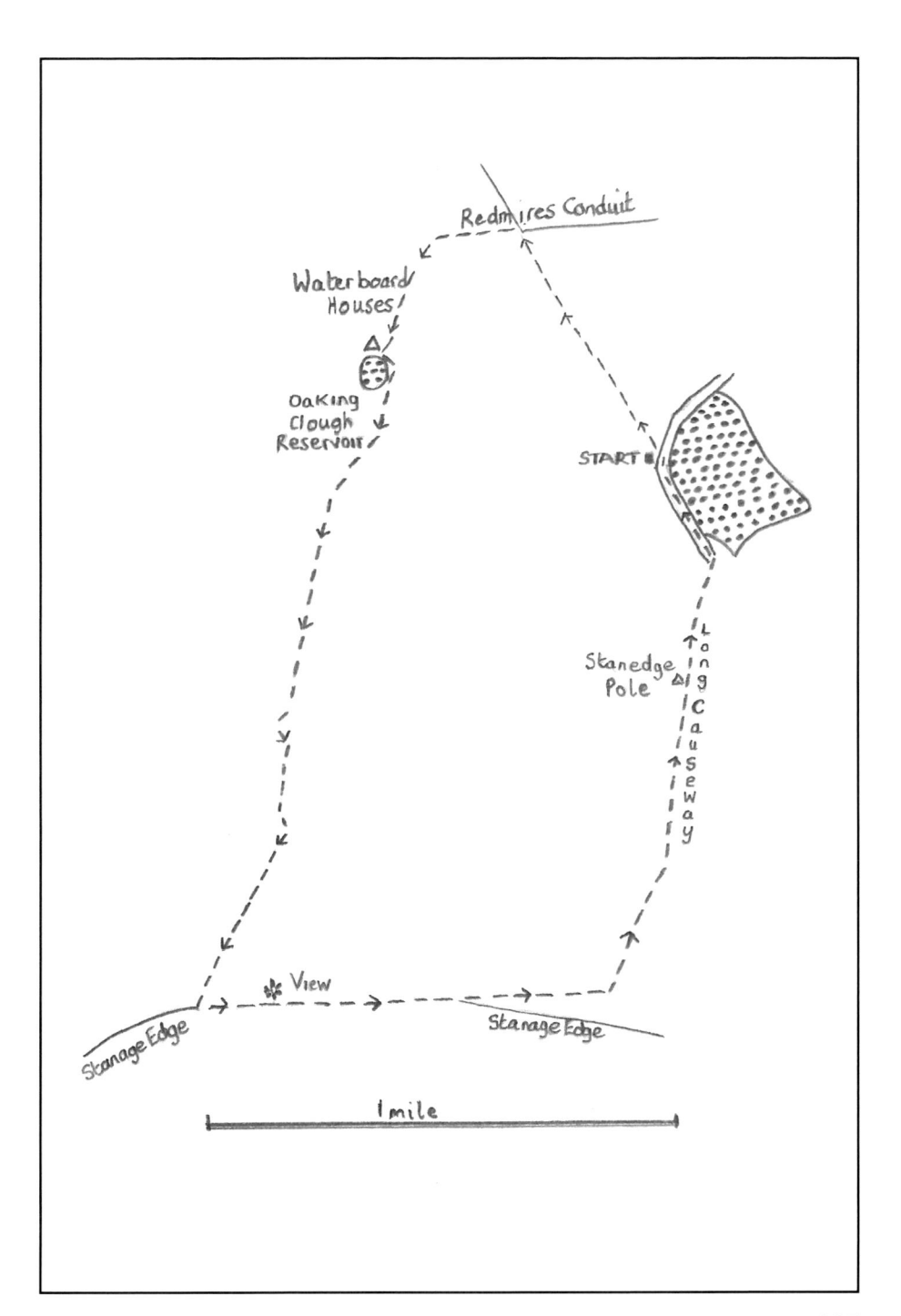

Walk Difficulty

Over Hallam Moors the ground is uneven and can get very muddy, as can Stanage where there could also be standing water. But with no great hills, and only a couple of stiles this isn't too difficult a walk.

Starting Point

The starting point for this walk is the Upper Redmires Reservoir Car Park, Long Causeway, S10 4QZ. If the car park is full, there is on-street parking close by.

The Route

Leave the car park at the opposite end to the entrance on to a path leading up a banking. Stay on this path across boggy ground for ¾ of a mile keeping in the same direction to reach a path crossing left and right. Go left over a stile next to a gate to follow Redmires Conduit to its start.

Reaching the reservoir, go right across a bridge to visit the old houses, then return back to the path to take a path on the left just after the sluice gate and keep on it to reach a stream after a few minutes. The path becomes a little vague after crossing the stream as it heads uphill to a small wood enclosed by a wall. Go to the right of the wood, keeping the wall on the left until the enclosure ends.

Here, go through a gap in the wall then after 15 yards take a track to the right with the wall now on the right. Keep on this track as it steadily climbs uphill with the wall on the right all the way. At the top of the hill, about a mile after crossing the stream, as the path bends to the left towards a large house, take an obvious track going to the right.

Passing numerous grouse butts, after half a mile pass to the left of a hut and reach the top of Stanage Edge. Turn left to walk along the top of The Edge all the way to where it joins Long Causeway coming from the right. Keep on the Causeway as it leaves the Edge, and after passing Stanedge Pole, the path leads on to Redmires Road at its starting point. Turn left to walk along the road to the car park.

Look out for…..

Oaking Clough Reservoir. The reservoir was built in the early 1800's to supply water to the growing town of Sheffield. The conduit was built at the same time and ran for just over 6 miles to reservoirs in the Crookes area.

Waterboard houses. The houses were built by Sheffield Waterworks in the early 19c. The larger room was lived in by the Spillway Keeper and the smaller room was lived in by the man who walked the boundaries and banks. Poorly paid and fed, the people who lived there relied on coal and food supplies being brought to them by packhorse or mule along a pack way down from Stanage Edge.

Stanage Edge. Stanage was used in some scenes in the 2005 remake of Pride and Prejudice. Access to the Edge however was not always as open as it is today. Stanage used to be a private grouse moor with gamekeepers often bribed to allow access to rock climbers in the 19th century.

Long Causeway or **Long Causey** is 2.5 miles long and was a Medieval packhorse route which ran between Sheffield and Hathersage. In the past the route has been marked on maps as a Roman Road and it is believed it was part of the Batham Gate route between Templeborough and Buxton.

Stanedge Pole. An ancient way marker which marks the boundary between Derbyshire and South Yorkshire. It stands at 438 metres, 1437 feet. It has been there since 1550, and due to its deteriorating state was replaced in April 2016.

Dog Suitability

For most of the walk there could be sheep, so dogs will need to be kept under close control. They can be off lead on the conduit and also on the last part of Long Causeway approaching the upper reservoir.

Refreshments

There is nowhere on the route to obtain refreshments, but there are shops and pubs in Lodge Moor, and the Norfolk Arms at Ringinglow is not too far away either.

Walk No: 23 Ladybower 'Lost Villages'

7.5 miles / 4 hours

Introduction

When the Derwent Valley was flooded to create the Ladybower Reservoir two small villages were lost beneath the water. Occasionally during drought periods remains from the villages appear, and on this walk the route passes close to where the villages were. On mainly good paths, starting from the Moscar area, the walk takes a gentle route to reach Cutthroat Bridge and then on to the Ladybower Inn and the first 'lost' village of Ashopton. From there the walk leads alongside the reservoir for a mile and a half to the remains of Derwent Village before returning to the start by climbing up to Derwent Edge, and then crossing Derwent Moor. The height gain from the reservoir to the high point of the walk is 244 metres (800 feet).

Ladybower Reservoir from Derwent Edge

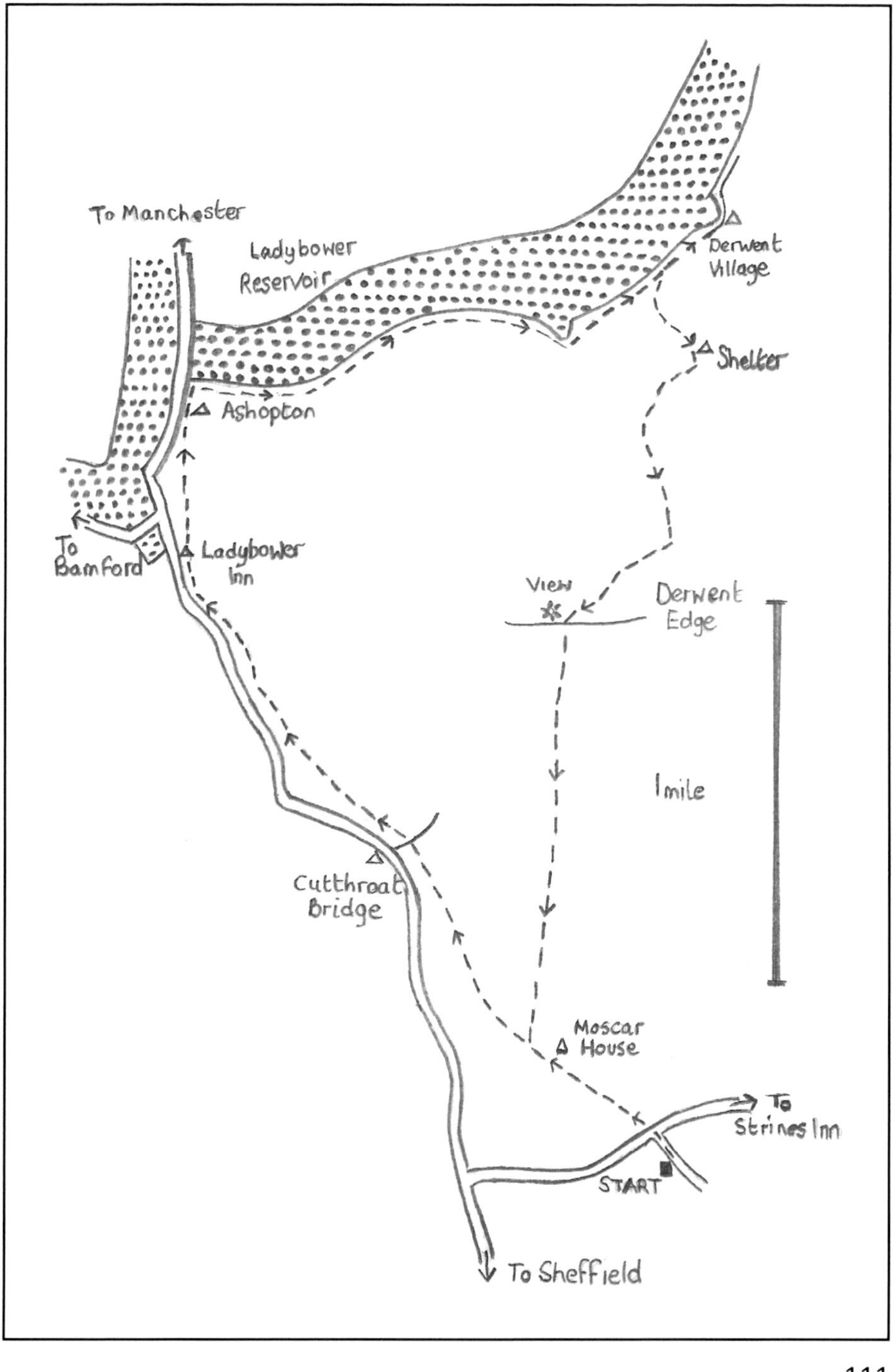
To Manchester
Ladybower
Reservoir
Derwent
Village
Shelter
Ashopton
To
Bamford
Ladybower
Inn
View
Derwent
Edge
1 mile
Cutthroat
Bridge
Moscar
House
To
Strines Inn
START
To Sheffield

Walk Difficulty

The most difficult part of this walk is the climb up from the reservoir to Derwent Edge. Crossing the moors has its ups and downs on the rocky paths, and there could be the usual mud and standing water after rain, but on the plus side there are only two or three stiles on the walk.

Starting Point

The walk could be started from Ashopton Viaduct, which would cut about a mile from the length of the walk, but because the parking area there is so popular, for this book the starting point chosen is a roadside area where there is more likely to be room to park. This is at the bottom of Sugworth Road close to where it meets Mortimer Road. The postcode for a house opposite is S6 6JA.

The Route

Walk down to Mortimer Road and cross to a path opposite which leads to Moscar House. Pass through the farm buildings and about 400 yards further on ignore a path right to go over a stile to carry on in the same direction. Close to the A57 at Cutthroat Bridge the path drops down a banking to cross a small stream. On the other side go right at a 'T', then soon after a few yards take a path left which tracks the road. After just under a mile the path passes behind the Ladybower Inn then after another half a mile the path reaches a gate with buildings on the right. Ignore a path right and take the driveway to the left which passes between a few houses in Ashopton.

Quarter of a mile along this driveway where it goes sharp left to the road, go straight on through a gate to walk on Derwent Lane alongside the Ladybower Dam. After 1.4 miles the lane reaches a gate on the right. This is where the route goes after a quick visit to the site of Derwent village. So ignoring this path right for time being, stay on the lane for a further ¼ mile to a point to where the lane bends left. Just here on the left there is a sign with information about Derwent village, and if the water is low it is possible to walk on the water's edge amongst ruined buildings.

Returning to the gate passed a few minutes earlier, go through it to bend right and then left as it leads uphill to a couple of barns and a shelter.

After crossing a stream the path carries on climbing uphill on a walled track to start with, before carrying on through open moorland until just under a mile from the bottom it reaches a 'T' junction of paths. Turn right here, then after 20 yards take a path left to carry on to the top of the hill. Go straight across at cross paths to follow a line of grouse butts for a while until after just over a mile the path walked earlier in the walk close to Moscar House is reached. Turn left here on to the path leading to the House, and then back to the start.

Look out for…..

Cutthroat Bridge where in 1635 an unknown traveller was discovered with his throat cut. He died two days later without either his or his murderers identities being discovered. In 1995 a Sheffield man Anthony Antoniou and two accomplices beheaded Antoniou's stepfather then dumped the body at Cutthroat Bridge, burying the head in Bedfordshire.

The Ladybower Inn dates back to 18c and was once used as a morgue during a spate of local murders in the 1700s. The culprit was never found!

Ashopton or what's left of it. The main part of the village sat under where the viaduct now is and whereas the remains of Derwent are visible when the water levels are low, Ashopton will never been seen again as silt has covered the remains of the buildings. When it was destroyed Ashopton had a population of around 100 people and had a village inn, post office, a hall, and a chapel.

Derwent Village which had two churches and a manor house. After demolition, the church steeple stood defiantly out of the water for some time before being dynamited four years later.

Dog Suitability

Across the moors there could be sheep so the usual rules about dogs being under control apply, but Derwent Lane is perfect for dog walking.

Refreshments

The start of the walk is close to the Strines Inn, otherwise it's a small diversion to the Ladybower Inn for refreshments.

Walk No: 24 Rivelin Valley

4.5 miles / 2.25 hours

Introduction

This is a great walk for people who are interested in Sheffield's industrial history. Evidence of the industrial revolution and how it affected Sheffield is everywhere. There are numerous water wheel sites, dams, a couple of quarries overlooking the valley and an ancient packhorse route to seek out during the walk. There are also some amazing views of the Rivelin Valley to enjoy in the first part of the walk from the packhorse track as it rises high above the valley. There is also an interesting story about a former inn too. This is quite an easy walk as the climb up the valley side is pretty steady, and there are only a couple of stiles along the way too.

The River Rivelin in full flow after heavy rain

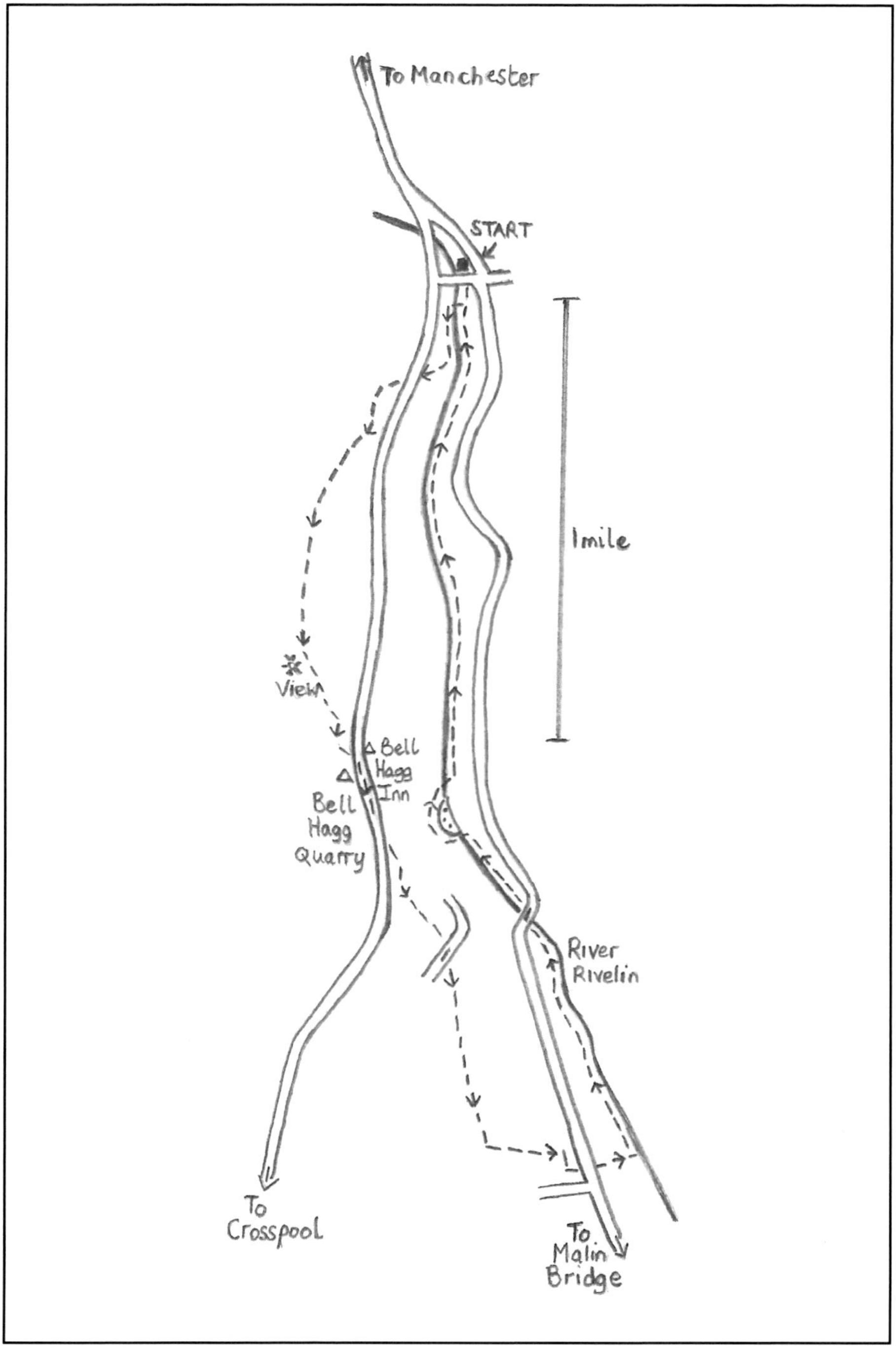
To Manchester
START
1mile
View
Bell Hagg Inn
Bell Hagg Quarry
River Rivelin
To Crosspool
To Malin Bridge

Walk Difficulty

There is a tricky set of steps heading down to Bell Hagg quarry, and some paths which have steep drops alongside them, but apart from the chance of a lot of mud on the valley paths, that's it on this walk.

Starting Point

Rails Road car park, Rails Road, Sheffield S6 6GF

The Route

From the car park cross the road on to a path opposite, then after a few yards cross a stone bridge on the right. Stay on this path as it goes left through trees and then forks right to reach Manchester Road. Turn left to walk along the road for a few yards to cross the road to take a track opposite. The track climbs ¾ mile heading towards a stone house in the distance. Just before the house, take the signposted path on the left to circle round the house. Once round the house the path very quickly reaches steps which lead back down to Manchester Road. Cross over and walk along the road for around 400 yards to 2 footpath signs on the left just before a 30mph sign.

Take the right path to walk through an old quarry with a steep drop on the left. Leaving this area go straight on at cross paths with a fence on the right to start with. Staying on the top of a cliff with more steep drops go over a stile into a field, to head to the bottom corner of the field. Once through trees go over a stile on the left in a second field on to a path which goes right to reach a lane. Walk along the lane for 30 yards to take a footpath sign on the left. Stay on this path for 400 yards as it rises slightly and ends at a wall.

Through the wall turn left to walk downhill with trees on the right, and the wall on the left. At the bottom of the hill the path bends right into the trees. About 30 yards before this path reaches Hagg Hill turn left at a footpath sign to come out on to Rivelin Road. Cross the road then walk along it for a few yards to take a footpath on the left which leads down to the river.

Turn left on to the footpath along the river then after ¼ mile at a fork take either option as they join back up a bit further on. Just after the next dam the path reaches the road. Cross to the right, taking the second path then after a further ¼ mile the path reaches Hind Wheel Dam. Go to the left of the dam and stay on this path as it stays next to the river.

After ¾ of a mile it reaches a clearing on the right. Just after the clearing there are two options. Going left leads down to stepping stones and a footbridge to cross the river twice. Taking the right fork leads uphill towards the road, but 30 yards before reaching the road there is a path left to go down steps which lead back down to the river to carry on in the same direction. Both paths meet up here and after 300 yards reach the car park.

Look out for…..

Rivelin Valley Trail which is 2 and a half miles long and runs from Malin Bridge in Hillsborough to where Rivelin Valley Road meets Manchester Road.

Coppice Road an old pack horse route used by quarry workers who took stone from the Bell Hagg quarry.

Bell Hagg Quarry which was worked to remove ganister and sandstone from a thick layer of millstone grit. Sandstone was used for stone bricks, kerb stones, cobbles and setts used in road and yard construction. Ganister is used in the manufacture of silica brick typically used to line furnaces.

Bell Hagg Inn built in 1832 by Dr Hodgson a successful gambler who called his house Hodgsons Choice, and later on, Hodgsons Folly. Hodgson built the house to antagonise the Vicar of Stannington after he turned down a generous donation because he had made much of his fortune from gambling. The house became a pub in the early 1900's and closed in 2005.

Rivelin Valley Industrial ruins. In its heyday in a three-mile stretch of the river the valley had 21 mill dams and 20 waterwheels providing power for the steel and cutlery industries, forge, paper mills and corn mills. The last waterwheel ceased operation in 1885 as waterpower gave way to steam, and larger-scale production moved elsewhere in Sheffield.

Dog Suitability

This is a good walk for dog walking, as apart from the crossing roads dogs can be off lead all the way through the walk.

Refreshments

The excellent Rivelin Park café and The Rivelin pub are the nearest places to get refreshments on this walk

Walk No: 25 Strines & Dale Dyke

7 miles / 4 hours

Introduction

Starting from the Moscar area of Sheffield this Peak District walk is quite an easy but rewarding hike which takes in high moors and two iconic reservoirs above the village of Bradfield. Strines reservoir and Dale Dike, famous for the 1860's Great Sheffield Flood figure prominently in this walk, as do Sugworth House and Boots Tower which are also on the route. Using mainly farm tracks and field paths there can be a lot of mud in winter and after rain, so stout boots are a must. Great views and a sense of being away from it all are what can be expected in this quiet area for walkers.

Bridge crossing the Dale Dike feeder stream in autumn

To Strines Inn

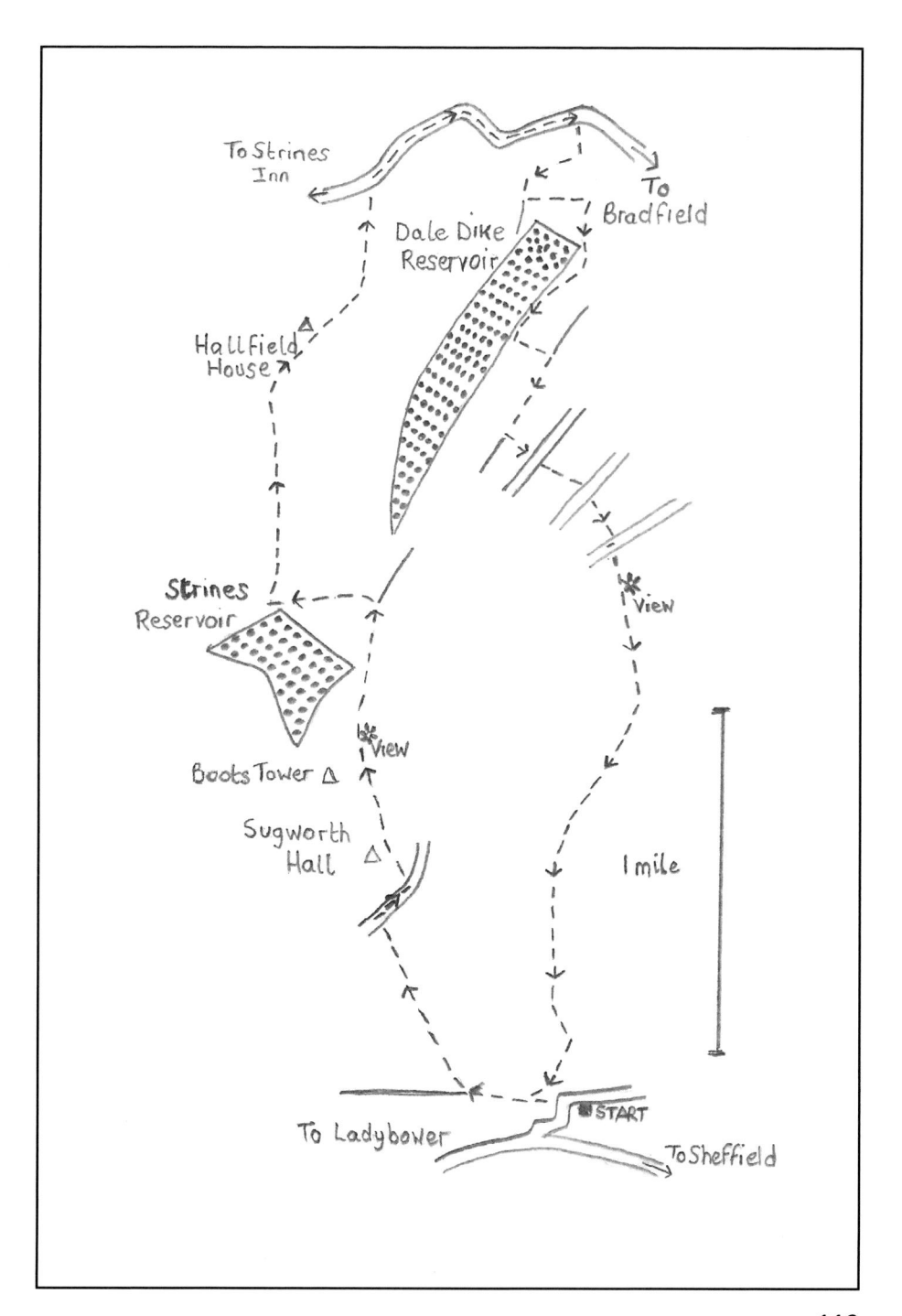

To Bradfield

Dale Dike Reservoir

Hallfield House

Strines Reservoir

View

Boots Tower △

Sugworth Hall △

View

1 mile

To Ladybower

START

To Sheffield

Walk Difficulty

On the first part of the walk there are a couple of boggy sections, then after that it's mainly decent paths although there are a few of stiles to negotiate. There is also a 10-15 minute climb from Dale Dike up to Ughill Moor.

Starting Point

The walk starts from a small parking area on Rod Side at Moscar. This spot can best be found by driving to Centre Barks kennels, Hollow Meadows, Sheffield S6 6GL, then with the kennels on the right, taking the next road right after about 200 yards. This is Rod Side. The parking area is ¼ mile along here, at the second right bend.

The Route

At the road bend close to the parking area take a track opposite. Ignoring a track joining the track from the right, after just under half a mile take a path right before the farm. Keep on this path until it reaches Sugworth Road, then turn right to walk along the road for about 200 yards to reach the entranceway to Sugworth Hall. Go through a stile to the left of the gates and head down the drive for about 100 yards. A footpath on the right heads through a rhododendron tunnel to enter a field with Boots Tower ahead.

After a visit to the tower return to the path and at a fork take the left path which descends the field with Dale Dike reservoir ahead. Once through this boggy section head for the bottom corner of the field to go over a high stile at a wall. After going over the stile turn left then where the path splits just before the stream take the left fork to cross over a wooden bridge.

Climb the bank towards cottages which are next to Strines reservoir. After passing the cottages take a farm track right which after just over half a mile reaches Hallifield farm. The path here diverts right to skirt the farm then continues for a further 0.4 of a mile to reach Dale road. Half a mile along this road go through a gateway on the right at a footpath signpost.

As the path heads towards Dale Dike reservoir take a path left which winds its way down to a bridge crossing a stream. At the other side, take the path up the steps and then follow the path alongside the reservoir for ¼ mile before taking a path left over a stile to enter woods. This path goes uphill to reach a track. Turn right on to the track then after ¼ mile the path leaves the woods at a wall. Through the wall turn immediate left to start the uphill climb.

With the wall on the left, after a short while cross a road to walk along fields in the same direction to reach another road. Cross this to a path almost opposite and carry on once again in the same direction on the edge of woods to reach a third road. Turn right here to walk along the road for about 100 yards to take a track on the left to cross Ughill Moor. After 1.5 miles the track reaches the track used at the start of the walk. Turn left for the parking area.

Look out for…..

Sugworth Hall, originally built in the 1600's the hall was extended by Charles Boot, the son of Henry Boot in the 1900's. The name Sugworth is derived from Anglo-Saxon words sugga (soggy) and worth (settlement).

Boots Tower was built in 1927 to provide work for Henry Boots workers during the depression. It is thought that it was built for Henry Boot to see his wife's grave in the churchyard at High Bradfield.

Dale Dike Reservoir which is well-known for the Great Sheffield Flood of 1864. On the 11th of March that year the newly built dam burst causing one of the biggest man-made disasters in British history. The escaping water rushed down the Loxley Valley and into the River Don with 240 people in total losing their lives. There was no gradual escape of water but a "sudden and overwhelming rush", and the reservoir was empty in 47 minutes, with water cascading down the hillside at speeds of up to 18 mph. In the following hours, the settlements of Bradfield, Damflask, Little Matlock, Loxley, Malin Bridge, Owlerton and many others, as well as the houses, farms, and mills in between, were swept away by the raging water. The reservoir was rebuilt in 1875.

Strines Reservoir which was built in 1871 and is the smallest of Bradfield's four reservoirs.

Hallfield House, a Grade 2 listed building which was mainly constructed in the 1600's although there has been a house on the same site since 1300.

Dog Suitability

Mostly, the tracks are sheep-free but there could be cows and sheep near Boots Tower. At Dale Dike dogs can be off-lead too.

Refreshments

Unfortunately there is nowhere for refreshments anywhere near this walk. The nearest pubs are at Ladybower 3 miles away and Dungworth 4 miles.

An empty looking Strines Reservoir in November 2018

Walk No: 26 Brookfield Manor

4.5 miles / 2.5 hours

Introduction

There is some lovely countryside between Hathersage and Stanage, with rolling hills, woodland, parkland and always the looming ridge of Stanage Edge high above giving it a magnificent backdrop. There are also some intriguing names on this route too such as Dennis Knoll, Cogger's Lane, Baulk Lane, Cottis Side and Bronte Cottage. This walk starts on the old roman road Long Causeway beneath Stanage, and using little-used paths and tracks winds its way almost to the village of Hathersage. Here is an area called Outseats which the route passes through to reach the Brookfield Manor Estate. From there its tracks and moorland paths and a visit to an old mill site to return to the start. This is a fairly easy walk but some of the paths can get very muddy after rain and in winter.

On the way to Outseats

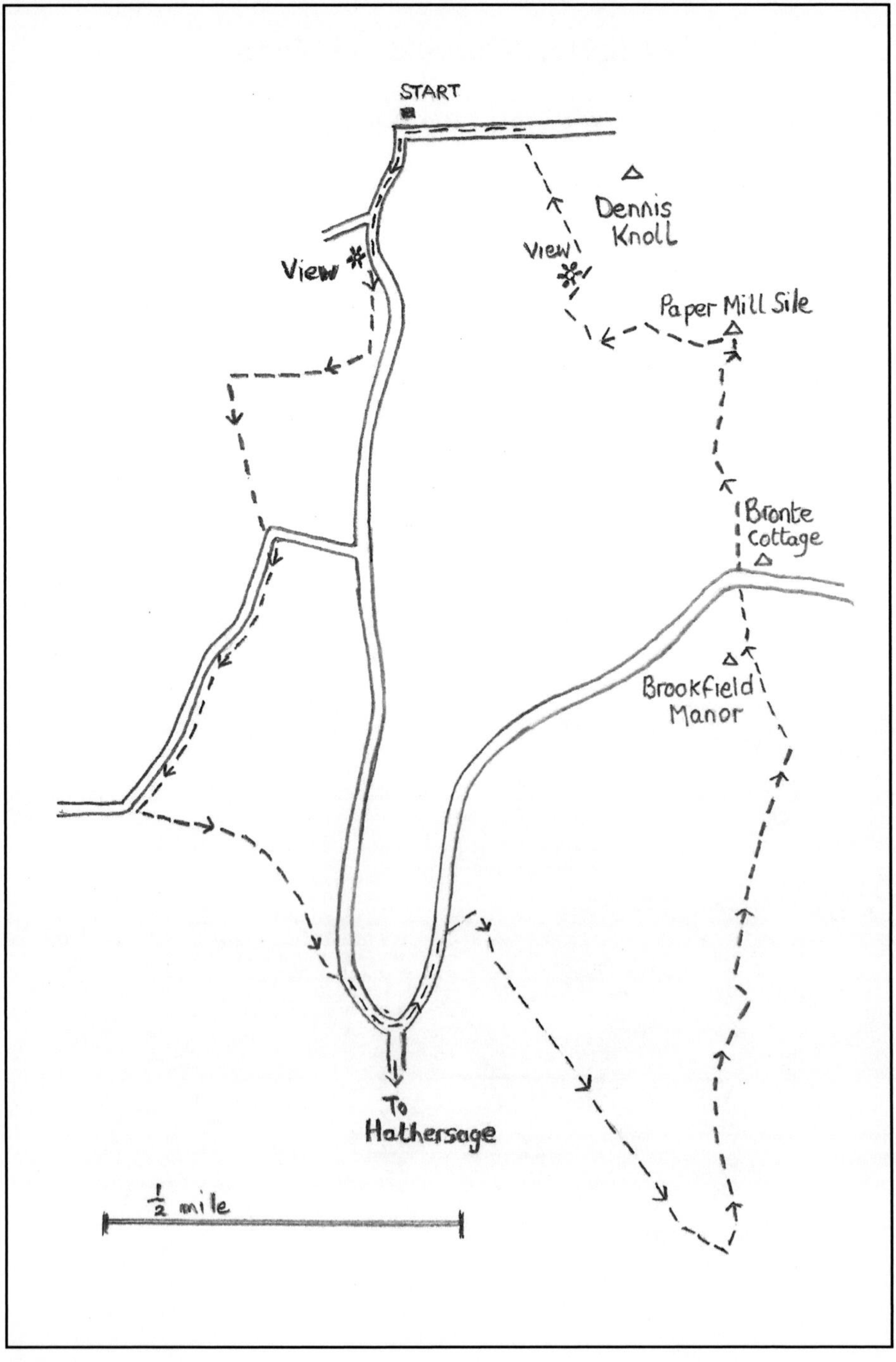
START
View
View
Dennis Knoll
Paper Mill Site
Bronte Cottage
Brookfield Manor
To Hathersage
1/2 mile

Walk Difficulty

There are quite a few stiles on this walk, some difficult, and overhanging branches to watch out for but there are no great hills en route.

Starting Point

Dennis Knoll car park is the starting point for this walk. The car park is in a pretty remote area, situated at the junction of Long Causeway and North Lees. The postcode is S32 1BQ but as this may cover a large area it may be best to check where the car park is on a map before setting off.

The Route

From the top of the car park go round the bend in the road and on to Long Causeway. Walking along the road, after passing a road on the right, about 200 yards further on take a path on the right. Ignore a path right leading to a small quarry to bear left on to a path which bends right below a small hill and enters a narrow wood. After passing a fork right, take a stile over a wall on the left at a signpost. Cross three fields and stiles keeping in the same direction downhill, then 2 more stiles through scrubland to reach a road.

Turn right along the road for 50 yards then go through a gate on the left on to a path which runs parallel to the road. After a short while the path comes back on to the road for a few yards before leaving it again to carry on in the same direction. At the end of the next field the path comes back out on to the road at the entrance to Nether Hurst Farm. Cross over the drive to go through a gate on the left to track the road again through 2 more fields.

After going through a gate at the bottom corner of the second field take a path going 90 degrees left between hedgerows. Further on the path becomes a track and passes between a bunkhouse and farm buildings. At the farm drive, take a stile opposite into a field. Turn right to walk next to the hedge then after crossing a stream in the bottom stay to the right to go uphill for 40 yards to a stile on the right just after a gate. Over the stile, keep to the left of the field to reach a road. Turn right along the road for 75 yards then at a junction where the old school was situated, go left to pass Birley Farm.

Immediately after passing the farm go over a stile on the right which skirts round the farm to reach a stile on the left. The path enters a field and keeps to a fence on the right in a field, then enters woods before cutting diagonally across a grass banking to reach Brookfield Manor drive. There is no clear path here, but the route keeps in the same direction to cross more grass to soon reach a brook. Across the brook the path turns right to go over a stile. Turn left here to go through allotments to Baulk Road.

Turn left along the road which becomes a track keeping more or less in the same direction heading towards Brookfield Manor. Ignoring any paths right, after half a mile as the track approaches housing ahead take an obvious path left which passes to the right of the Manor via an enclosed path. A field path then leads to a road with Bronte cottage to the right. Cross the road to a path opposite to go through a field which is often very boggy, and head towards the woods ahead. In the woods ignore a path left and after about 350 yards the path is joined by a path coming from the right to cross a stream on the left on stepping stones. In front is the site of Green's House Paper Mill.

Turn left to come out of the woods into fields which lead to Green's House and farmhouse. Passing through the houses take a path on the right which heads uphill. After the path bends right keep straight forward alongside a wall ignoring a gap in the wall and a stile on the right until after 0.4 of a mile a gate on the right is reached, just before trees. Through the gate turn left to reach the road, then left again to return to the car park.

Look out for.....

Geer Green School site on Coggers Lane. In 1718 Benjamin Ashton of Hathersage made a grant of £200 to buy land at Outseats "for the building of a public school to benefit the poor of Hathersage and Outseats". The school consisted of a schoolroom and 2 small rooms at one end. In 1804 a larger school was built in Hathersage and three years later Geer Green closed.

Brookfield Manor dates back to 14c. It was extended around 1825 when it was given a gothic façade and is now in the private ownership of Sir Hugh and Lady Sykes. Civil weddings are held there, and there is also a conference centre. Brookfield Manor was 'Vale Hall' in the book 'Jane Eyre' written by Charlotte Bronte when she stayed with her friend at Hathersage in 1845.

Green's House Paper Mill site where wrapping paper for the needles and pins that were famously produced in Hathersage in the 19c was produced. The mill dates back to the 1840's but ceased production before the end of the 19th century. High behind what's left of the old buildings is a natural dam and millpond which still discharges water beside walling where the waterwheel was situated.

Dennis Knoll is an area to the right of the plantation situated on the left on the final path of this walk (see map). There is speculation that due to the amount and type of man-made cairns (mounds of rough stones built as memorials or landmarks) and a pre-historic field system found there, that Dennis Knoll was a Bronze Age settlement. (3000-1200 BC)

Dog Suitability

There are long stretches of this walk where there may be farm animals so it's not really a suitable walk for dogs to be off lead, unless they can be kept under close control.

Refreshments

Hathersage is the nearest place for refreshments where there is a good choice of pubs, cafes and shops selling food and drink. There is also the Norfolk Arms at Ringinglow not too far away from the start of the walk.

Walk No: 27 Chatsworth

7.5 - 8 miles / 4 hours

Introduction

There are two good looks at Chatsworth House on this walk, one from the river on the first part of the walk, and then a second one at the old stable area on the way back. This is a fairly easy walk on mainly good paths and tracks entirely within the Chatsworth Estate and includes an optional look at the village of Edensor as well. Starting from Baslow, to begin with the walk follows the River Derwent past the house all the way down to Calton Lees garden centre before crossing the bridge on to a road opposite which leads steeply uphill to open moorland with great views across the valley. From there, a track high up in the woods leads to Swiss Lake and Cottage, before the route heads off down to the side entrance to the house, via the Hunting Tower and the old aqueduct. Then it's back to Baslow via the river path again.

The House from the river path

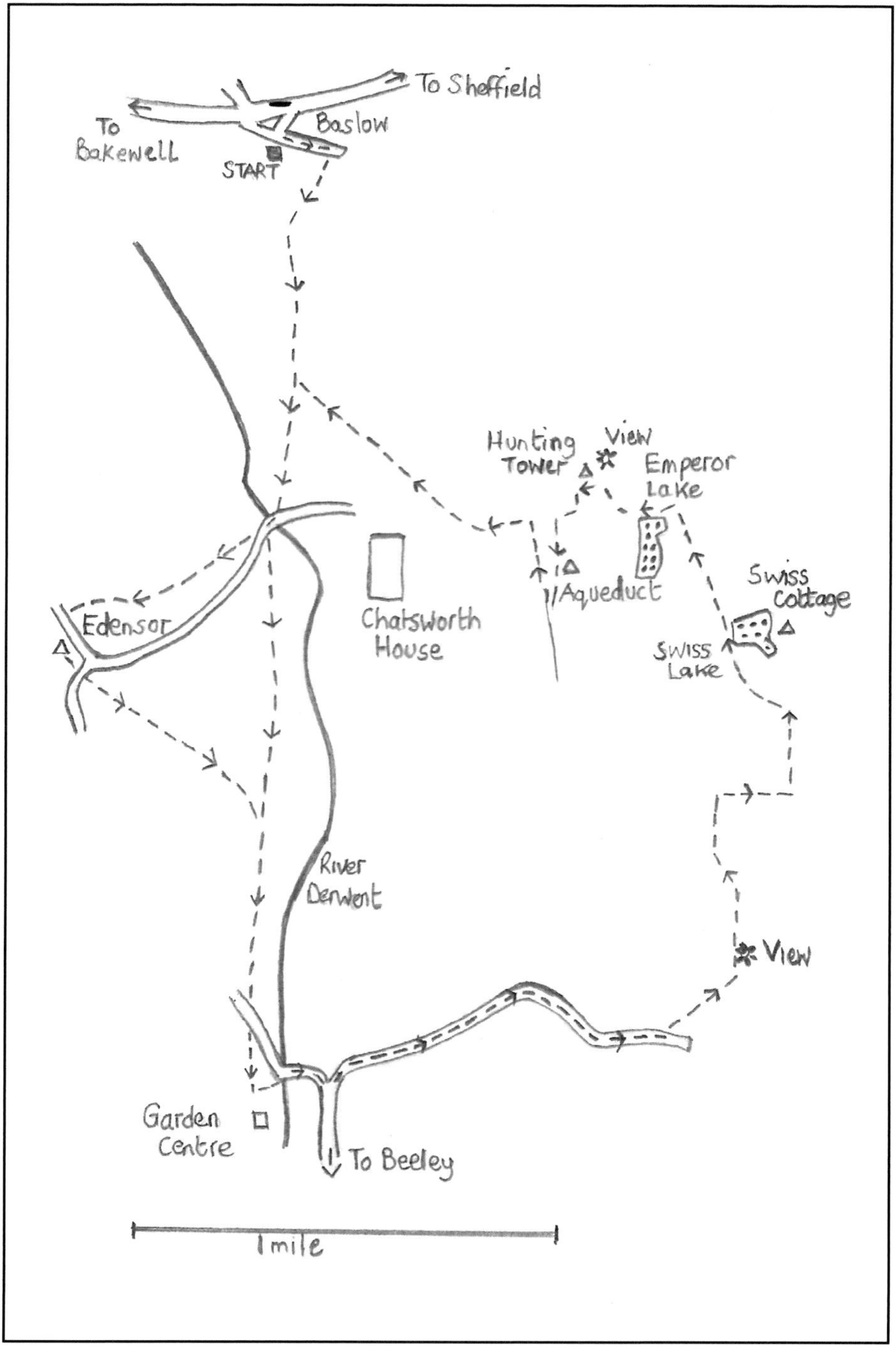

To Sheffield
To Bakewell
Baslow
START
Hunting Tower
View
Emperor Lake
Aqueduct
Chatsworth House
Swiss Cottage
Swiss Lake
Edensor
River Derwent
View
Garden Centre
To Beeley
1 mile

Walk Difficulty

The steep uphill section is the main difficulty on this walk and a lot of people might not be capable of a steep one mile climb. The views from up there are worth the effort though, and apart from the possibility of mud in a few places, that's it for hazards on this walk.

Starting Point

The walk starts at the car park in the centre of Baslow in Church Lane, postcode DE45 1SS

The Route

From the car park turn right along Church Lane then immediately after crossing the bridge take the lane on the right which quickly becomes a path. After going through a kissing gate, keep on this path alongside the river to reach the road which leads to the house. Turn right to cross the bridge, then at this point either head half right across the right to have a look at Edensor village, or turn left to walk alongside the river. If viewing Edensor, return to the river path afterwards.

There are two choices of paths along the river which meet back up further along. Where they meet, go up steps on to a path which leaves the river and cuts across grass to reach the estate road. Go left for a few yards then cross to go through a gate leading into a car park. Head through the car park and on to the garden centre access road. If refreshments are needed from the garden centre carry straight on, if not, take a path left just before the garden centre car park leading down through woods and back to the estate road.

Cross the river bridge and stay on the road for 100 yards, then as the road bends right, take the road left ignoring the track on the left leading to the house. This quiet road soon leads uphill, and further up becomes a track. After half a mile, just after passing a farm on the right, take a signed path on the left which initially goes through a field before cutting diagonally across moorland to reach a ridge. Turn left here to head towards woodland.

Over a stile into the woodland the path becomes a wide track and turns right a couple of times and left a couple of times until after just under a mile it passes to the left of Swiss Lake and Swiss Cottage. After a further ¼ of a mile the track bends left as it crosses a stream which opens up to the left to enter Emperor Lake. After ¼ of a mile the path leads down to the Hunting Tower.

After visiting the tower, leave from the path opposite the front door to go down some steps on to a track which goes left. After passing the aqueduct, the track reaches another track going left and right. Turn right and stay on this track as it goes downhill to reach various estate buildings. After bending left the track reaches a car park with the old stables on the left. Carrying on downhill, pass the house on the left, and then cut across parkland on the right to re-join the river path back to Baslow.

Look out for…..

Baslow village green. Unlike the Yorkshire Dales, and elsewhere in the country, there are very few villages in the Peak District which have village greens. Eyam, Parwich, Ashford-in-the-water, Litton, Monyash, Foolow are the others.

Edensor. In the 18c, most of Edensor was clearly visible from Chatsworth House. When the 4th Duke remodelled the estate, he decided to clear away all the village houses that interrupted his view over the park. The 6th then created a brand new village that would be out of sight of the house. Park Cottage in the hollow is commonly thought to have been saved during the demolition of the old village as it could not be seen from Chatsworth House, but some people believe that it was spared because the Duke did not want to disturb the occupant, who was suffering from typhoid.

Swiss Lake which was built in 1710 to provide water to the house. It obtained its name in 1839 when Swiss Cottage was built.

Emperor Lake which was built in 1845 to feed Emperor fountain in the gardens at Chatsworth.

The Hunting Tower built in the 1570s and was sited on the crest of the hill to provide extensive views of the deer park, both for locating deer, observing the hunting, as well as being a place for banquets.

The Aqueduct which dates from 1839 when Joseph Paxton designed the pools and fountains at Chatsworth for the 6th Duke of Devonshire. It formed part of the flow of water that supplied the Cascade at the House. It is believed to have been inspired by a similar much larger structure in Germany.

Dog Suitability

There are sheep and deer throughout the river section of the walk, but once the moorland section is reached dogs can be off lead most of the way back.

Refreshments

As well as the many pubs and cafes in Baslow there is Calton Lees Garden centre and the stables area at Chatsworth for refreshments.

The ruined Aqueduct which often has water running over it after rainfall

Walk No: 28 Wyming Brook

4 miles / 2 hours

Introduction

Often referred to as 'Little Switzerland', Wyming Brook is a gem of a place, and less than 5 miles from Sheffield city centre, it is another Sheffield beauty spot which is also within the Peak District. On this walk, starting at the top of Wyming Brook the route quickly leads across Hallam Moor to a section of the Redmires Conduit to enjoy great views towards the city. Then it's a path through moorland heather to walk along a delightful stretch of the River Rivelin for a while before joining up with the no longer used Wyming Brook Drive to reach Wyming Brook itself, and the climb back to the start. Walking up Wyming Brook, crossing the bridges with water crashing all around is a delightful experience, and is the highlight of the walk. This walk can be quite tough in places including a couple of tricky sections before the rocky climb up Wyming Brook is made, so stout boots are a must, especially in winter.

Wyming Brook bathed in sunshine

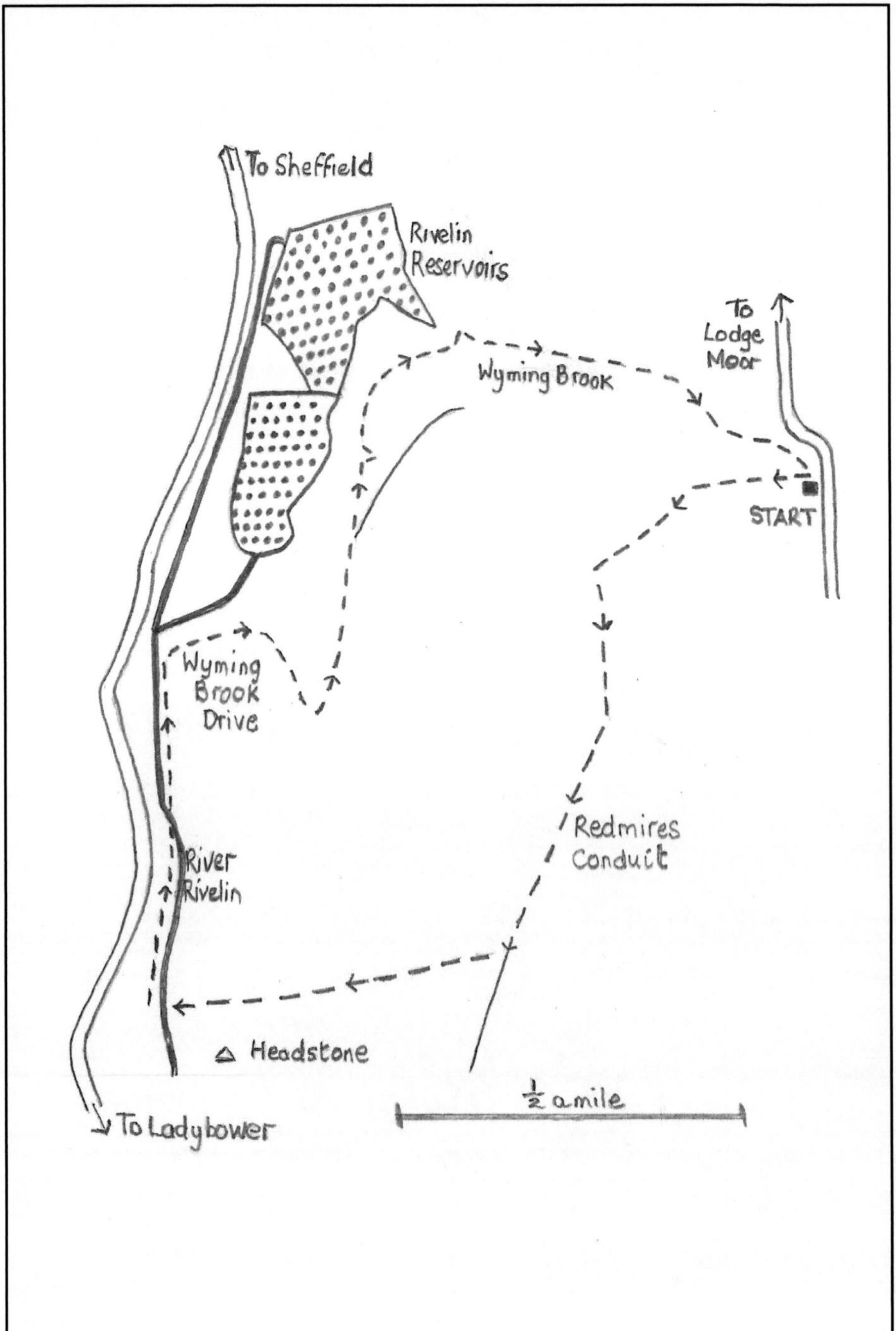
To Sheffield
Rivelin Reservoirs
To Lodge Moor
Wyming Brook
START
Wyming Brook Drive
Redmires Conduit
River Rivelin
Headstone
½ a mile
To Ladybower

Walk Difficulty

Two potentially very boggy sections at the start of the walk are followed by a tricky downhill section to get to the Rivelin. Tree roots and uneven paths along the Rivelin are followed by the path up Wyming Brook where there are rocks to climb, and often mud and standing water.

Starting Point

Wyming Nature Reserve Car Park, Redmires Road, S10 4QX. The postcode for the car park may cover a wide area in which case an easier way to find the start point is to find The Three Merry Lads pub, Redmires Rd, Sheffield S10 4LJ, and the car park is ¾ of a mile past the pub on the same side of the road.

The Route

In the car park, take a signposted path up a banking. The path goes through a wooded area alongside a wall, and where the wall ends go through a gate to take a path leading half left. The path goes through heather to pass through a boggy area and trees, then keeps in the same direction to reach a broken wall. Through the wall turn left to go uphill to reach Redmires Conduit.

Turn right along the conduit, and after about half a mile at cross paths next to a bridge go over a stile on the right on to moorland to head down to the River Rivelin. Keep on this path as it heads through a boggy section to reach cross paths where the Headstone rocky outcrop can be viewed on the left. Carry on in the same direction through a steep section to reach a bridge.

Over the bridge turn right to follow a rough path which stays to the left of the river all the way to a large stone bridge. Turn right to cross the bridge on to Wyming Brook Drive and keep on this disused road until just after a mile it reaches a fork. Take the downhill fork to the left and after about 10 minutes turn right at a public footpath sign to enter Wyming Brook Nature Reserve.

Stay on this footpath through the Nature Reserve crossing numerous bridges until as the path approaches a clearing there are two choices at the last bridge. Crossing the bridge leads to stepping stones back over the brook to get back to the car park, or taking a path straight ahead stays to the right of the brook and leads back to the car park that way.

Look out for…..

Redmires Conduit which was built in the 1830s to supply water to Sheffield. It taps the source of the River Rivelin out on the moor and bends round the side of the hill to bypass the Redmires dams before heading off to Lodge Moor. At that point it disappears underground.

The Headstone is a large naturally occurring upright block of grit stone surrounded by a sea of smaller rocks. Due to the many fractures in the rock and viewed from the right angle it appears to have facial features.

Wyming Brook Drive which was built by unemployed labour during the depression of the 1920's and was one of the most picturesque drives in the area when motoring was in its infancy.

Wyming Brook which was once set aside for the exclusive use of the nobility when it was part of the hunting and hawking grounds of Rivelin Chase. It is now a Site of Special Scientific Interest (SSSI) and is a wooded ravine with a crystal-clear brook tumbling through it. Passing over mossy stones and part-submerged tree roots the brook is criss-crossed by a series of picturesque wooden footbridges on its' dramatic route.

Dog Suitability

The only part of the walk where dogs need to be led is the half mile section between Redmires Conduit and the Rivelin where there might be sheep.

Refreshments

The 3 pubs on Redmires Road in Lodge Moor are the Three Merry Lads, the Shiny Sheff, and the Sportsman. There are also shops selling drinks and snacks on Rochester Road in Lodge Moor.

Walk No: 29 Win Hill

7 miles / 4 hours

Introduction

Win Hill is an iconic Hope Valley landmark, which at over 1500 feet above sea level can be seen and identified from miles away because of Win Hill Pike, referred to locally as 'The Pimple', which lies on top of it. There are fantastic views on all sides once up there, and for this walk the approach to it is made from the lesser-used Ladybower side of the hill. The route used includes passing Bamford Mill at the start of the walk, and then after walking a section of the Thornhill Trail, there's a quick look at the Ladybower Reservoir before starting the long climb to get to the top. The return leg is a nice, steady descent through the village of Thornhill. This is quite a strenuous walk and is probably more suited to experienced walkers.

Win Hill looking beautiful in the snow

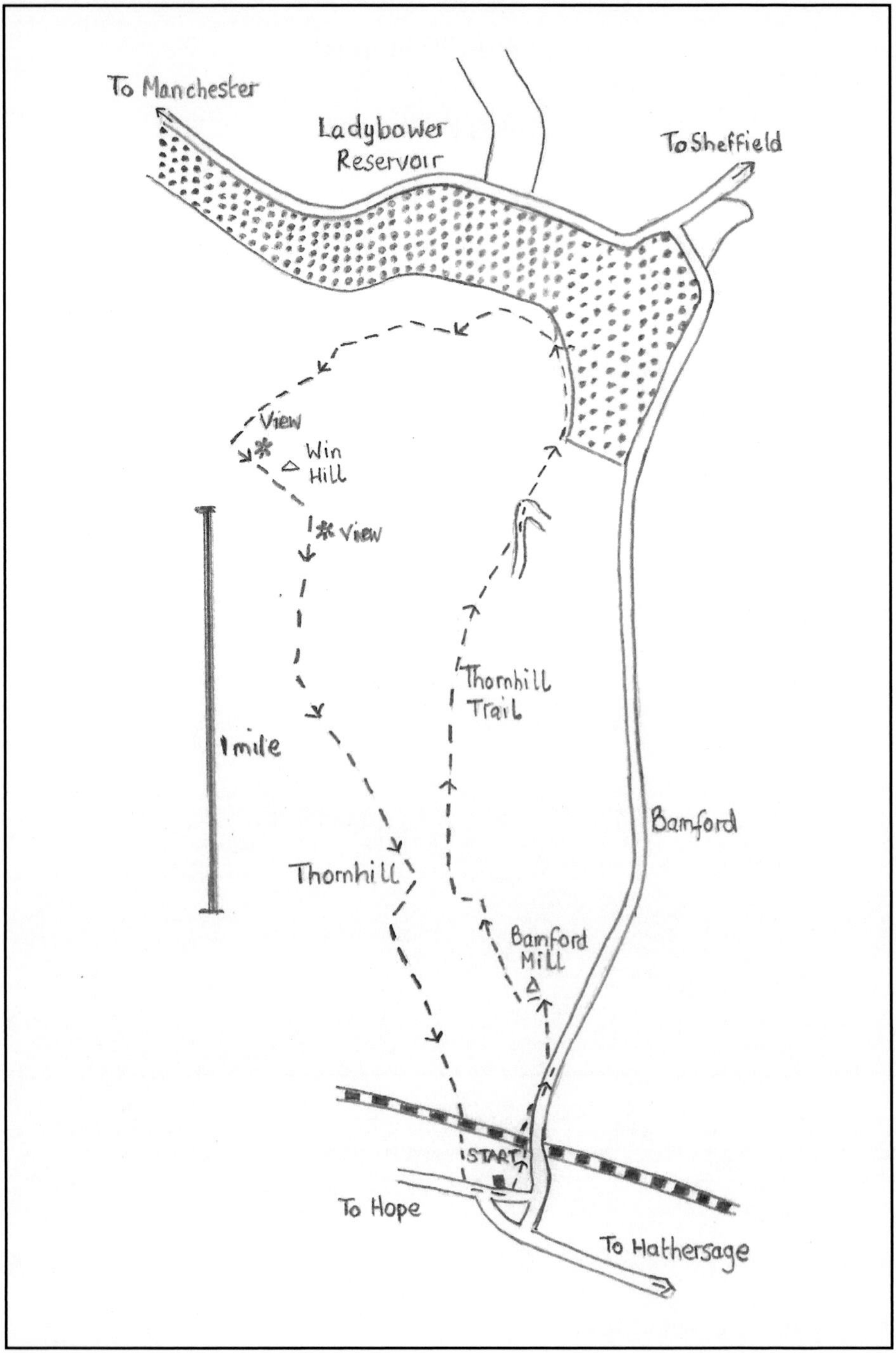
To Manchester
Ladybower
Reservoir
To Sheffield
View
Win
Hill
View
1 mile
Thornhill
Trail
Bamford
Thornhill
Bamford
Mill
START
To Hope
To Hathersage

Walk Difficulty

Climbing more than 1300 feet is the main difficulty on this walk, and not only does the climb getting steeper the nearer it gets to the top, it also becomes quite rocky up there too. Care needs to be taken coming off the top as well as there are loose stones to contend with as well as the steepness of the paths.

Starting Point

Mytham Bridge is the starting point chosen for this walk as there is plenty of roadside parking there. Mytham Bridge is the name of a road in Bamford and the postcode for it is S33 0EA.

The Route

Walk back up Mytham Bridge from the bottom to take a stile on the left on to a path which leads into a campsite. Take the road through the campsite which comes out on to the main road, then turn left to walk towards Bamford. Approaching houses, turn left on to Mill Lane keeping on this road as it passes the mill. Just before the road becomes a track turn left at a path signpost, and then 50 yards on, left again to cross a weir and a river bridge to go into a field. Go half right in the field to head for the top right corner, then after passing through a gate keep in the same direction to enter another field.

Go through 2 more gates, then at a finger post go left uphill to go through another gate to reach Thornhill Trial, a disused railway track. Turn right to walk along the track, staying on it for just over a mile as it crosses a minor to reach a second minor road further up. Turn left to walk up the road to Ladybower dam wall. Walk on a path alongside the dam for about a third of a mile to take the second path left, leading uphill.

Ignoring a track left and a path right keep going uphill in the same direction. After about 100 yards a path left leads to a ruined house which is a good place to have refreshments. After visiting the house, return to the path and carry on uphill. Soon, the path comes out of the woods to reach a wire fence. Go left alongside the fence and at a corner climb over the fence to go through a gate on the right.

At a signpost on the other side of the gate there is a very steep path left which is the more direct way to reach the summit. An easier, and more enjoyable way to reach the summit is to go straight forward here, and further on, it is possible to take an approach to the summit with views on both sides. So, going straight forward through heather, with the wood on the right the path leads to a signpost after a few minutes. Turn left at the signpost to follow the sign for 'Hope' to go uphill with Winhill Pike to the left. Reaching the ridge go left to get to the top and after taking in the views from the top carry on in the same direction to go down the other side towards woods.

After about a quarter of a mile the path reaches a junction of paths in the woods. Turn right alongside a wall then after about 550 yards go left at a Thornhill sign. The path descends in the same direction and after 275 yards reaches another signpost at a wall. Turn left along the wall to a gate. Pass through the gate and follow the path to the south-east for 400 yards where numerous paths go off in all directions. Ignoring paths left and right follow a well-defined path downhill which leads on to a country lane.

At the end of the lane go left at a 'T' junction, then right at the next 'T'. 80 yards down this road take a path on the left to carry on downhill to reach the old railway track. Go right to the end of the track then turn left along a lane for 50 yards to take a stile right which crosses a field to reach a railway. Go under the railway bridge and carry on straight forward to reach the main road then turn left to return to the start.

Look out for.....

Bamford Mill which was built in 1782 as a water powered corn mill. 9 years later, after being destroyed by fire it was rebuilt as a cotton mill. In the early 19c it was converted to steam power and by 1857 the mill employed 230 mill hand. Owners Courtaulds closed the mill in 1965 after which it was used in the manufacture of electric kilns and laboratory furnaces until it was closed permanently in the 1990s to become private residences.

Win Hill, where allegedly there was a battle in 626 when the armies of Wessex and Mercia fought the army of Northumbria. Outnumbered, the Northumbrians were facing defeat until they managed to crush their rivals (literally) by rolling boulders on to them from the top of the hill.

Thornhill Trail dates to the early 1900's when a seven mile stretch of railway was laid from a junction at Bamford station to help in the building of Derwent and Howden dams. Once complete, thousands of tons of stone were transported from a quarry near Grindleford to the construction sites further up the Derwent Valley. The route was open for 13 years during which time it transported more than a million tons of stone from the quarry to the work site. In 1916 Derwent Reservoir was completed and the track was lifted.

Dog Suitability

On the section towards the top of Win Hill there are sheep so dogs must be led there, but for the rest of the walk dogs can be off lead.

Refreshments

Apart from pubs and shops in Bamford a short drive away, the petrol station at Sickleholme has a shop for refreshments, and there is also the excellent café at the Hope Valley Garden Centre at the start of the walk.

Crook Hill and the Ladybower Reservoir looking from Win Hill Pike

Walk No: 30 Bradfield

4.75 miles / 2.5 hours

Introduction

A fair amount of climbing early on in this walk makes it tough going at the start, with an ascent of around 400 feet from Low Bradfield to get to the high point of the walk near Castle Hill getting the heartrate going somewhat to say the least. Once up there, the views are worth the effort though, looking both across the Loxley Valley, and also up towards Dale Dike Reservoir. Using little used paths from the start, the route then leaves Castle Hill to take in High Bradfield and St Nicholas Church there before heading off to Agden Reservoir and lovely paths round the reservoir to return to the start. There are a range of different paths on this walk starting with field paths, then farm tracks, woodland paths, more field paths before the walk ends with the reservoir path and a bit of road walking.

Approaching High Bradfield from Bradfield Brewery

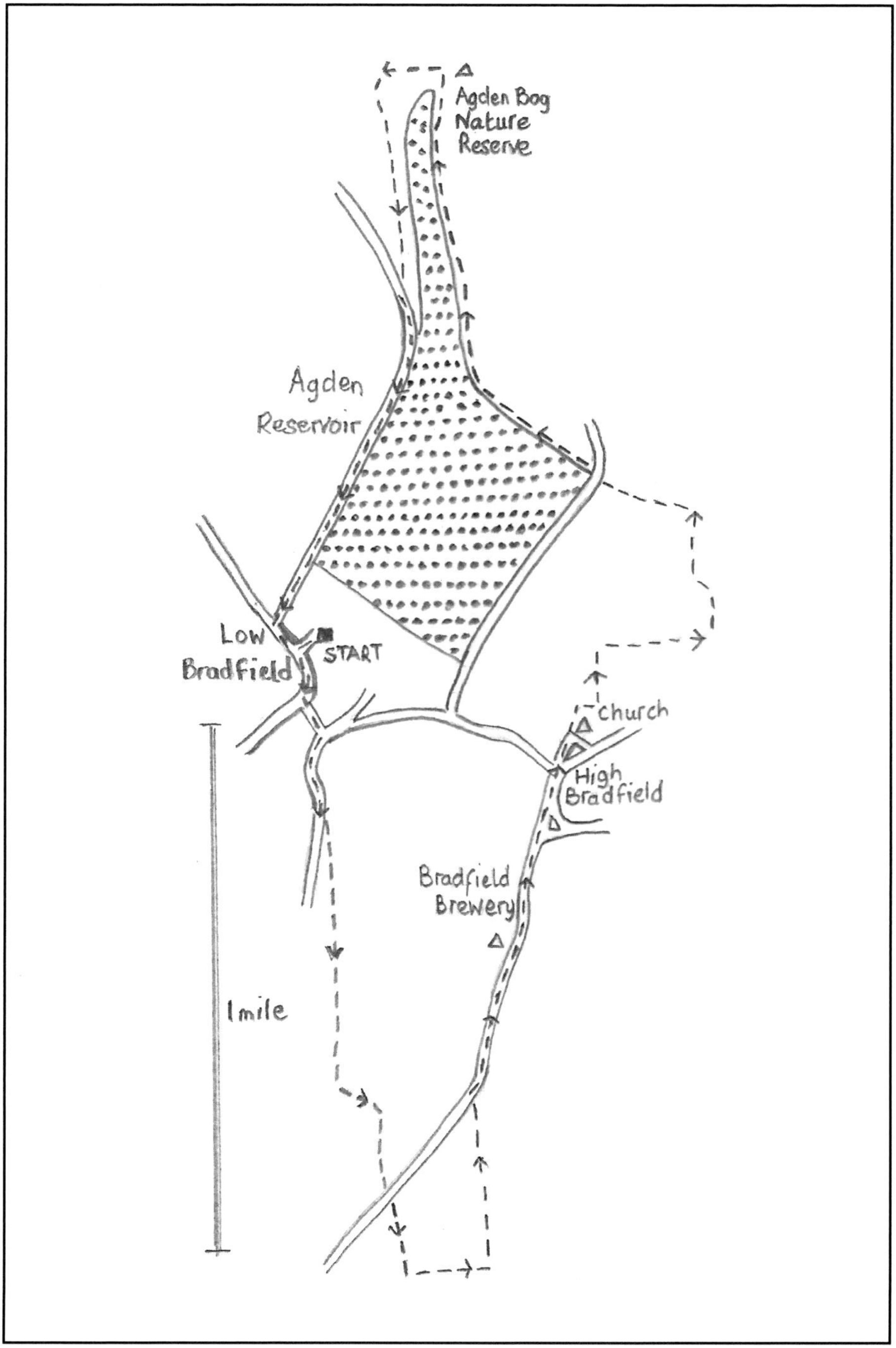
Agden Bog
Nature
Reserve
Agden
Reservoir
Low
Bradfield
START
Church
High
Bradfield
Bradfield
Brewery
1mile

Walk Difficulty

The climb at the start is strength sapping but should be within the capability of regular walkers, and there is only one difficult stile as most other stiles have been replaced by gates. There could be a lot of mud through the fields and on the farm tracks, and there is one short section near St Nicholas Church to watch out for where there is a steep drop on one side. The only other thing to watch out for is tree roots on the path round the reservoir.

Starting Point

The starting point is The Sands car park, Low Bradfield, S6 6LB but there is also roadside parking in the village where the walk could also be started.

The Route

From the car park return to the road, go left, then left again over the bridge which crosses the river. After a few yards turn right on to another road and then after 150 yards at a footpath sign go left up a farm track. As the track levels go through a gate on the left to go above the farm. The path carries on uphill to go through three more gates keeping in the same direction, then in the next field cross to a gap in the wall on the other side of the field about 30 yards from the bottom.

In the next field head for a gate in the top right corner. Through the gate there is a grass mound straight in front. Keep below it to go round it, then at a broken wall at the top of the field look for a stone stile to the left to climb over ruined stones to reach a short, enclosed path behind the wall. Through a gate the path goes right and leads to 2 more signposted gates.

Through the second gate head uphill to a footpath signpost keeping to the right of a wall. Through a squeezer stile head diagonally across the next field to a marker at a gap in a broken wall. Cross the final field in this section to reach a metal gate in the top corner to go on to the road. Cross on to a farm drive opposite and stay on the drive as it goes uphill through a farm smallholding, and then bends left to keep going uphill to reach another track at the top going left and right. Turn left here to return to the road.

Turn right to walk along the road into High Bradfield and go straight across to the church yard. Pass the church then go right and left still within the churchyard to leave it at a kissing gate. A few yards further on ignore paths left and right to go on to a path at the same level to start with, with a steep drop to the left. After the path bends left and goes downhill to a stream, cross the stream to take a grassy lane left.

After going round a bend, after 100 yards there are two sets of old gateposts on the right just before a paths junction. Take the right one to go up a banking then after 20 yards take a path left through a wall to go straight across on to a wide grassy path. The path stays at roughly the same level with Rocher Edge above on the right until after about 300 yards it reaches a small ladder stile over a wall on the left, just before a fenced off marshy area. Go over the stile to head for the left side of a row of trees straight ahead. Go through trees and down a banking on to a path leading towards a road.

Go left along the road for a few yards then immediate right on a path alongside the reservoir which winds through trees and stays close to the water. 50 yards before the path reaches a metal fence take an unsigned path right which leads up to a track to carry on in the same direction. It is easy to miss this path so if this happens, just turn back and have another look for it, on the left now! Back on the track after a few minutes ignore a small bridge down below on the left to stay on the track until it crosses a stone bridge.

At the other side, the path bears left to climb steadily away from the water through a nature reserve. At the top, where the path levels it reaches a track going left and right. Go left to walk along the track for just under half a mile until it joins up with a road going in the same direction. Walk along the road for just over half a mile to reach a 'T' junction. Go left, then next left leads back to the car park.

Look out for.....

Bradfield brewery a family concern which in a little over 15 years has gone from milking 100 cows a day to brewing over 100,000 pints of beer a week!

St Nicholas Church, one of only five Grade I Listed buildings in Sheffield. Parts of it dates back to 1109 but the majority of it was added in 14c and 15c.

Agden Bog nature reserve, a classic example of a type of bog that has mostly disappeared from our landscape following draining of the land for farming.

Dog Suitability

The fields to start with could have sheep in them, so dogs on lead would be the advice there, but the rest of the route is perfect for off-lead walking apart from the church section and the small amount of road walking at the end.

Refreshments

There are 3 great pubs, The Plough, The Horns and the Nags Head, all serving Bradfield Brewery's Farmers Ales which are also available at the brewery shop. There is also a local shop/café in Low Bradfield.

Autumn scene at Agden Reservoir

147

Sheffield and Peak District Walking Group

All the walks in this book are walks that have been put together for our walking group. Altogether we have over 100 walks and are still adding to the total to make sure that we're not forever repeating the same ones.

Although some of the walks we do are only 4 miles long, there are very few of the walks which don't have some type of challenge in them. Whether this is a steep hill, lots of stiles, muddy paths or rocky sections varies from walk to walk. One thing we like to do though is not rush, and make sure that we enjoy our surroundings as we walk along.

New members are always welcome, but we do ask that when people come on the walks that they wear adequate clothing and footwear, and bring sufficient food and drink for the duration of the walks.

We are currently arranging on average 2 walks a week all year round and below are details of what to expect on our walks.

Morning walks – at the moment these are taking place on Fridays and Saturdays, usually twice a month on both days. They are normally 4-5 miles long, and last 2 – 2.5 hours. The usual meet up time is 9.15, but sometimes we arrange what we call 'Breakfast walks' where we meet up at 7.45 and bring some food with us to have a breakfast stop at around 9.

Sunday walks – these are full day walks and again we normally meet at 9.15. They usually take between 4 and 5.5 hours and are 7- 10 miles long. Experienced walkers are most suited to these walks.

Evening walks – are either sunset, twilight or torch walks depending on the time of year! At the moment these walks take place on Tuesday nights, once or twice a month.

For more details, email **sheffieldandpeakdistrictwalks@gmail.com**

The Countryside Code

Respect other people
- Consider the local community and other people enjoying the outdoors
- Park carefully so access to gateways and driveways is clear
- Leave gates and property as you find them
- Follow paths but give way to others where it's narrow

Protect the natural environment
- Leave no trace of your visit, take all your litter home
- Don't have BBQs or fires
- Keep dogs under effective control
- Dog poo - bag it and bin it

Enjoy the outdoors
- Plan ahead, check what facilities are open, be prepared
- Follow advice and local signs and obey social distancing measures

Enjoy, be safe

About the Author

Steve and his wife Andrea live in the North of Sheffield where they have both lived all their lives. Steve's passion for walking started as a boy when in his own words "we used to walk everywhere", including long Sunday family walks. For most of his adult life he has been a dog owner, and taking his dogs for long walks, and also enjoying walking with his family as they were growing up prepared him for the more serious walking which he has enjoyed since 2006. This was the year that he joined a fledgling walking group which had about 10 members and walked most Sunday's. Pretty soon, the two leaders had left the group, and Steve volunteered to arrange and lead the walks, and has been walk leading ever since. Along the way he trained as a Walking for Health leader, and also became a leader trainer, training other leaders. Since 2015 he has been employed by organisations such as Sheffield International Students, the Crisis charity and the Norfolk Arms at Ringinglow to lead walks on their behalf, but more recently with Andrea's help he has branched out to run his own walking group, the Sheffield and Peak District Walking Group.

Away from walking Steve enjoys most sports, especially cricket, football and rugby and loves music, especially watching live bands at pubs and clubs in Sheffield. Also, reading and socialising are an important part of his life, as are his daughters and grandchildren.

When asked to name a favourite place to walk, Steve has preferred to mention a few places that are special to him, although some of these places will have to wait until Volume 2 to be included! Wharncliffe Crags was a regular place for his family to go as a child, so he says that it deserves a mention along with other Sheffield favourites, Wyming Brook, the Porter Valley and Bradfield. Meanwhile in Derbyshire Lathkilldale, Castleton and Dove Dale are the favourite ones there. Further afield, many a walk on the Cornish Coastal path has been enjoyed, and Wharfedale in the Grassington/Kettlewell area including Malham Cove is much-loved too. In Wales, Steve says that walking Mount Snowdon and Red Wharf Bay in Anglesey takes some beating for him and in general, strolling along a canal or river anywhere, especially if there is a nice pub, is just the ticket!